The Big Win

*Learning from the
Legends to Become a More
Successful Investor*

Stephen L. Weiss

WILEY

John Wiley & Sons, Inc.

Published by John Wiley & Sons, Inc., Hoboken, New Jersey.
Published simultaneously in Canada.

For general information on our other products and services or for technical support,
please contact our Customer Care Department within the United States at (800)
762-2974, outside the United States at (317) 572-3993 or fax (317) 572-4002.

Wiley also publishes its books in a variety of electronic formats. Some content that
appears in print may not be available in electronic books. For more information
about Wiley products, visit our web site at www.wiley.com.

Library of Congress Cataloging-in-Publication Data:
Weiss, Stephen L., 1955—
    The big win : learning from the legends to become a more successful investor/
Stephen Weiss.
        p. cm.
    Includes bibliographical references and index.
    ISBN 978-0-470-91610-0 (cloth); ISBN 978-1-118-22127-3 (ebk);
    ISBN 978-1-118-23358-0 (ebk); ISBN 978-1-118-25971-9 (ebk)
    1. Investments—United States.   2. Portfolio management—United
States.   I. Title.
    HG4910.W3678 2012
    332.60973—dc23
                                    2012004093

10 9 8 7 6 5 4 3 2 1

To Lauren, Shelby, and Lindsay
My BIGGEST WINS

Disclosure

Data from various sources was used in the preparation of this book. The information is believed to be reliable, accurate, and appropriate, but it is not guaranteed in any way. The forecasts and strategies contained herein are statements of opinion, and therefore may prove to be inaccurate. They are in fact the author's own opinions, and payment was not received in any form that influenced his opinions. Stephen L. Weiss implements many of the strategies described. This book contains the names of some companies used as examples of the strategies described, but none can be deemed recommendations to the book's readers. These strategies will be inappropriate for some investors, and we urge you to speak with a financial professional and carefully review any pertinent disclosures before implementing any investment strategy. This book has been prepared solely for informational purposes, and it is not an offer to buy or sell, or a solicitation to buy or sell, any security or instrument, or to participate in any particular trading strategy. Investment strategies described in this book may ultimately lose value even if the opinions and forecasts presented prove to be accurate. All investments involve varying amounts of risk, and their values will fluctuate. Investments may increase or decrease in value, and investors may lose money.

Contents

Acknowledgments

It seems that no matter what I set out to do, my wife, Lauren, is the critical component in my getting there. Always a great sounding board, she is also a wonderful editor, excellent illustrator, and all-around good sport. As with most all else that I have accomplished, I could not have written this book without her partnership and love. As we came down to the finish line, Lauren was also finally willing to own up to the fact that our beautiful, incredibly intelligent daughters take after me more than her, but I think that had everything to do with how they approach their schoolwork, and my missing the submission date for this book, and nothing to do with their better qualities. My aforementioned daughters, Lindsay and Shelby, were very understanding about the time commitment required to write this book and their enthusiasm about the project kept me enthused as well. They promised me that they would read *this* one, but I'm not going to hold out too much hope. Susanna

Margolis once more proved herself to be the best of the best as far as editors and confidants go. My in-laws, Harriet and Irwin Karassik, and sister-in-law, Beth, who, in addition to being responsible for making Lauren the person she is, were incredibly helpful in providing feedback on each chapter. Debby Englander at John Wiley & Sons was again extremely supportive, patient, and encouraging. I appreciate her continuing to have faith in me and my ability to write another well-received investment book. I hope she's right. Thank you, Debby. The entire staff at Wiley makes my job as an author very easy; Kimberly Bernard, Donna Martone, and Tula Batanchiev were very helpful. My appreciation also extends to Andrew Stuart, my agent, for continuing to represent my nonfiction efforts and getting my work in print. And of course a special thank you to all those who so graciously allowed me into their lives: Lee Ainslie, Jim Chanos, Alfred Taubman, Chuck Royce, Marty Whitman, Don Peebles, Renée Haugerud, and Jim Rogers. These very successful individuals gave me as much time as needed and could not have been more open during the process.

S.W.

Introduction

If you have flipped open the cover of this book, or tapped the screen on your iPad or Kindle to arrive at this introduction, I hope you won't be disappointed by not having found another dry, dull how-to book on investing. *The Big Win: Learning from the Legends to Become a More Successful Investor* has been written to read like a collection of entertaining short stories while providing invaluable insights, culled from the experiences of some of the best investors in the business, that you can integrate into your investment strategy in order to drive greater profitability.

My first book, *The Billion Dollar Mistake: Learning the Art of Investing Through the Missteps of Legendary Investors* (John Wiley & Sons, January 2010), profiled 11 top investors, their life stories, their paths to success, and their biggest mistakes. While virtually all investment books lay out a step-by-step strategy that, if adhered to, will allow for the achievement of "financial independence" or "success beyond your wildest dreams"—sarcasm intentional—*The Billion Dollar*

1

Mistake is unique in its approach—focusing on what *not* to do. It is a "don't do what I did and get rich" kind of book. The mistakes in each chapter are the garden-variety missteps that we all make, investors big and small, the only difference being the number of zeros to the left of the decimal point. In fact, most professional investors assiduously relive their mistakes, dissecting them over and over both as involuntary penance and, more productively, in an effort to understand what went wrong so that it doesn't happen again. George Santayana put it best[1] when he said: "Those who cannot remember the past are condemned to repeat it."

This follow-up, *The Big Win: Learning from the Legends to Become a More Successful Investor,* possesses many of the same characteristics of my first book. In fact, I used the same criteria for selecting those profiled on the following pages: compelling life stories, awe inspiring financial achievements, and most important, investment philosophies that could be successfully and relatively easily assimilated by the average investor in order to achieve greater profitability. But I also wanted to add a touch of diversity to the investments I examined while ensuring that the underlying tenets of each strategy were transferrable to and from all asset classes including stocks, bonds, real estate, and commodities. And to really spice it up, I added one of the best short sellers into the mix, offering you, the reader, the opportunity to make money in any type of market—bull, bear, or sideways. Importantly, each chapter concludes with *takeaways* that make it easy to grasp how you can—in fact, should—take advantage of each lesson. As noted, the core principles of any investment discipline should be transferrable to different asset classes; there are many ways to generate return on your capital, and stocks may not always be the best vehicle for wealth creation. In fact, one of the professional investors featured herein remains skeptical of the ability to consistently generate return by owning any stocks.

Virtually all those included herein blazed new trails in finance: Renée Haugerud, a woman, is an extremely successful hedge fund manager, a minority class if there ever was one; R. Donahue Peebles is perhaps this country's wealthiest African American real estate developer; Martin Whitman was at the forefront of distressed debt investing; Chuck Royce, a pioneer as a value investor in small capitalization companies; Jim Rogers, a former partner of George Soros, was an early hedge fund innovator in commodities; Jim Chanos is perhaps the best short seller of all time; Lee Ainslie started out working for Julian Robertson at Tiger Management and now runs one of the world's largest equity hedge funds; and Alfred Taubman is a multibillionaire real estate investor and inventor of the modern shopping mall.

The Big Win examines the other side of the trade discussed in *The Billion Dollar Mistake*. This book illustrates what went right for the eight investors featured, explaining how they parlayed their personal strengths into fortunes. Each chapter provides an analysis of an investor's biggest win, not necessarily in terms of monetary gain, although that is also present, but rather in terms of an investment that epitomizes their style. The chapters conclude with a takeaway laying out the most important aspect of each legend's strategy.

I hope you will find this book informative and entertaining— learning by osmosis, so to speak—as you enjoy the personal stories of these individuals who all came from humble backgrounds to achieve great wealth and success. Most of all, you should come away from this book with an appreciation of how you can use your personal strengths to profit in any market in any asset class.

Note

1. George Santayana (1863–1952) was an American philosopher. Historians, librarians, and trivia experts have engaged in spirited debate over his exact words, but the meaning is very clear.

Chapter 1

The Legends
I Have Met

*A Behind the Scenes Look at
What Makes a Legend*

Writing a book is work, hard work at times. So why do it? Well, no one said that work can't be enjoyable and I enjoy writing. In some respects, writing fiction is easier because you can just make stuff up, which is great for people who drink a lot or use mind-bending drugs. Fortunately, or unfortunately as the case may be, I don't imbibe to excess with the former and have never partaken of the latter so I am left with an unimpaired yet fertile imagination that occasionally lets me down by being very infertile. Such is the difficulty with fiction: The occasional inability to create something from nothing and then having to toil laboriously to make it sound coherent and interesting. But, I write fiction because I enjoy letting my mind wander and putting those thoughts

5

down on paper, fictitious thoughts that no one can say are incorrect. I enjoy the vacation from reality.

Nonfiction, on the other hand, is easier on the creative engine in terms of developing the material. Sure, you still have to make the book interesting and entertaining, no doubt about that, or people may read the phone book instead, a literary tome that arrives free of charge. But with nonfiction, at least the track is already in place, the basic content available if you know where to get it. In fact, what I enjoy most about writing nonfiction is the process of gathering material. It provides me the opportunity to meet some of the best investors who ever put a dollar at risk and some of the best business people who ever sat in a CEO's chair. Getting to know them in a rather informal setting, exchanging thoughts and ideas, but most of all, listening to them tell their stories and espouse their philosophy on life, investing, and business—often overlapping thoughts—is what interests me. Then, when I sit down to pull it all together, I enjoy reflecting upon these conversations, discerning whether there is a causal relationship between the people they were, the people they have become, and their success; how their life stories have served to create their approach to investing. I enjoy breaking down each piece of their strategy and then putting it all together, crafting it into a story that culminates with a practical application. I am rarely at a loss for what to write about in my business books. If writer's block rears its ugly head in one chapter, I move on to another individual. With fiction, that's not possible since the story line has out be fleshed out and followed.

With all this in mind, the following pages tell the story of my selection process, how I approached each person about being in the book, and my impressions of them as individuals and professionals. The purpose of this chapter is to entertain, provide insight into these professionals as individuals, and painlessly pull together the commonalities that have made them successful and show how you can adapt these qualities into your investment style.

Wanted: The Truly Successful and the Truly Interesting

On the surface, many portfolio managers appearing on television are like the doctors you entrust your care to; some docs graduated in the top of their class, some barely made it through medical school in Guadalajara, but their grades are never included in the laminated diploma framed on the wall. It's sort of the same thing with portfolio managers—their record of performance is usually nowhere to be found on the television screen as they preach investment advice. So instead of focusing my search for candidates to interview on name value alone, I sought out individuals who had accomplished something special, who did things differently perhaps, who were pioneers, original thinkers, *and* had great performance. I wanted those who had a definable strategy. Most of all, however, those profiled in this book had to invest within a strategy that I could break down and relate to individual investors for them to assimilate into their market activities. The starting point was people whom I was somewhat familiar with—either personally or professionally.

When I wrote *The Billion Dollar Mistake*, I actually found it easier to find those who had committed a severe misstep than being able to source true outperformers; bad news always gets more press. I also confirmed something I had already known—that a lot of mutual funds with an awful lot of money are pretty mediocre performers. Few actually outperform the market. It was more difficult to get a bead on hedge fund performance, but I have pretty good access to various reports that provide return information. The problem with these individuals is that most of them did not want to speak on the record; it just was not worth it to them in the post-2008 environment where successful capitalists are treated as modern-day lepers. And most of these people did not need the publicity to raise assets or they already had accumulated significant wealth. What I had going for me was that I was somewhat of a known commodity from my regular appearances on CNBC and Bloomberg, my first book, and a two-and-a–half-decade career on Wall Street. Chances were that I knew someone who could vouch for me—it was a bit like playing six degrees of separation—and that got me in the door. It was important to them that they could trust that I would not tarnish a reputation they had built through many years of hard work, that they would be portrayed fairly. However, this book is not a commercial for any of these people; in fact, most of their funds are closed to new investors.

The first person to agree to cooperate was Alfred Taubman, the founder of shopping mall developer Taubman Centers. I was in Florida with some friends for a weekend of golf, and Taubman was kind enough to host our group of seven for a round at Trump International in West Palm Beach. We drove our rented Explorer up the long driveway that contained more exotic cars than either the garage of a Bahraini prince or of a platinum record selling rapper. I was fortunate to play in Alfred's foursome, and the first thing I noticed was that he had an incredible swing for an 86-year-old. My instinct was to turn my 9 iron on him for having cost me a small fortune by building and operating a high end shopping mecca close to my home, but he was far too nice to be the subject of my misdirected anger. My family, much to the delight of American Express and to the detriment of my savings, has spent significant time helping The Mall at Short Hills achieve unmatched sales per square foot. As the round went on and our strokes piled up, I discovered he was very good at math, but the advantage of shooting high scores was that it gave us more time to discuss his career and his philosophy on retailing and investing. Taubman is not only a top real estate developer and retailing expert but he is also an inventor, the inventor of the modern enclosed mall. He spoke about the precision required in his business, the attention to detail, to finances, and to creating a value proposition to draw tenants and keep them. As with most great business people, he was very detail oriented, focused on costs and driving revenue. We discussed the book I was writing, this book, and without hesitation he agreed to participate. He immediately offered the Irvine Ranch as his biggest win, aside from Taubman Centers, that is. But what he spoke about with more pride and excitement was what he was doing with stem cells and other medical research. After the first 10 holes, the skies opened and our foursome headed into the clubhouse. The others braved the elements and continued on. On the way in, Alfred stopped to say hello to David Koch, one of the wealthiest men in the world. I admit to being impressed. We continued to chat and I continued to learn. Sitting down to lunch, we spotted The Donald in the corner, but he was too busy to notice us at the time. I had met Trump at another golf course, Wing Foot in Westchester, New York, and I wondered if all he ever does is play golf; I am fairly certain he did not wonder the same about me. As for Alfred Taubman, between traveling to his many homes in the United States and Europe, his business interests, charitable endeavors, and his desire to spend time with his family, it would be a few months before we were able to get together again to drill down into his story and his biggest win. In the interim, I read his book, *Threshold Resistance*, and researched his story.

I reflected on my conversations with Alfred and came away with the following insights into this multibillionaire that took him from nothing to one of the richest people in the country. He was focused from day one on his pursuit of success, employing a skillset, architecture, as the tool to get him where he wanted to go. He was an entrepreneur and brilliant individual who saw a need in America and filled it. Away from Taubman Centers, he has had many successful investments, including Sotheby's and the focus of his chapter, the Irvine Ranch, a truly interesting story that provides many lessons. He also has a great sense of humor. As we discussed the challenging macro environment, he said he prefers one-handed economists. I looked at him quizzically, and he explained that such physically challenged forecasters would have to possess serious conviction in their views since they could not present an alternate proposal. I got it. On the one hand if this happens, then . . . , but on the *other hand*; actually, there would be no other hand. As I said, Alfred is a man of precision and humor.

Jim Rogers is someone I have admired for a very long time. I would doubt that anyone knows more about commodity investing broadly or has done it as successfully for as long; or has taken the time to travel to virtually every part of the world to flesh out the investment case in practical terms. He partnered with George Soros in starting Quantum Funds and retired early, an action I very much admire. But he never really retired; he just went into business for himself. I admire that too. Well, Rogers and I have the retiring early and going into business for ourselves in common but it would have been nice to also have had Soros as a partner in common, so I could have more fun with the other two. Two out of three is not bad, I guess. I had no idea how to contact Jim, so I Googled him and found his e-mail address. I sent a message describing my background and he responded almost immediately—from Singapore. We set up a time to speak by telephone; I believe 1900 hours was what we settled on (I guess that's how they tell time in Singapore). Never having had any military training, I counted out the hours on my watch just to be sure. Yup, 7 P.M.—got it. I called at the appointed hour and told him a bit more about the project and he was in. Since Jim had written a number of books, I was sure he felt sympathy for a fellow author. He agreed to schedule some time when he visited New York in a few weeks. A week before he arrived I received an e-mail suggesting we meet at seven in the morning in the gym at his hotel. This would have been the second gym meeting I had in my career, but after the first, which was an impromptu meeting with Lee Cooperman in Omega's gym, I vowed never to do it again; there are more productive ways to have a discussion. Instead, we agreed to meet in the hotel lobby at two o'clock. He was fairly punctual, arriving at the hotel with his accountant in tow. We shed the number cruncher, hopped into a black Lincoln Town car supplied by Fox News, and headed to their studio a few blocks away. Go ahead, he said, and our interview began as I put the tape recorder on the armrest between us and started to fire questions.

As someone under contract to CNBC, I took pleasure in having the competition pay for my transportation, and I felt like a spy behind enemy lines as I walked into Fox's building. We continued with the interview in the elevator, into the lounge, and into the make-up room. People dropped by to say hello and I got the feeling this was not his first media event (no kidding). We then moved into the studio for Jim to be interviewed by the Fox Business anchor. I recorded that, too. Another stop, this time at Reuters, I believe. From my own television appearances, I was recognized everywhere and felt bad about taking the spotlight from Jim. Well, not quite the spotlight, more like an occasional and polite nod from someone else in the trenches. After a few hours, I had to head to the CNBC studio and genuinely felt bad about it. Jim wanted to talk more and I wanted to listen more, so we agreed to set up a time to finish the conversation when he returned to Singapore after traveling to other parts of the world to give a speech and likely to explore a new investment opportunity. It was an incredibly enjoyable afternoon as I moved in the wake of his incredibly fast pace. He does not look 69 years old and sure does not act like it with a schedule of international travel that few could handle. The follow-up call was scheduled, but I blew it. That damn military time! I called him late and can tell you he does not suffer fools particularly well. Duly and deservedly chastised, we moved on and finished the interview.

When I asked for his biggest win he said "my children." Admirable, understandable, and endearing but I asked for his second choice because I was writing an investment book, not one on family values. I came away more convinced about the commodities boom driven by growing economies in China and India but not as sure of the timing. For Rogers, investing is a way of life, every day an opportunity to explore and observe socioeconomic behavior that can either support or detract from a thesis. From Yale to Oxford and every day in between, Rogers just never seems to stop learning. He is intense, but unless you screw up, as I did, that intensity never detracts from his southern grace. He is brilliant without any hint of condescension. But most interesting of all is that, having uprooted his family and moved to Singapore, he is living out his investment thesis.

As with the others, my first contact with Marty Whitman was by e-mail. I followed up with a phone call and spoke to Bridget Wysong, the director of public relations for his firm. She responded that Marty gets lots of requests but doesn't like to do interviews. I mentioned that I was an investor in one of their funds and that if he did not agree to meet with me I would redeem my money. Okay, I didn't say the last part but I actually was an investor at the time. I gave Bridget my pitch and she said she would get back to me. Subsequently, my editor at Wiley called and mentioned she had taken a referral call from Marty's office. Soon I received an e-mail saying that Marty would be happy to participate in the book. When I arrived, I was escorted into his office and was greeted by a casually attired man in tennis sneakers, sweat pants, and a golf wind jacket; I felt a bit overdressed. The recorder was turned on and the conversation began. It was a very interesting few hours. I had done my research beforehand, filling in the pieces of information that I did not know, but our conversation was like a history lesson. As he recounted the personal side of his journey and then moved on to how he sort of stumbled into distressed investing, I felt like a family member listening to the patriarch's life story. As befitting someone who wrote the seminal book on distress investing and has been an adjunct professor at Yale, Syracuse, and Columbia University Graduate School of Business, Marty is one hell of a teacher.

I was looking for a woman to include in *The Big Win* (see sidebar in Chapter 3), and found Renée Haugerud rather quickly, the pool of possible candidates insufferably small. Renée was guarded about participating, and our scheduled time to get together had been moved around a few times to accommodate her ever-changing cal-

endar, but eventually we met at five o'clock one afternoon. The idea
was that we would spend an hour or so and then reconvene at another
time. The hour turned into two, then three, and into the fourth. I
am convinced I suffer from undiagnosed ADD because after two
hours I am usually either nodding off or begging for mercy, but I
do not recall even once attempting to discretely twist my wrist to
steal a look at the time. I have been around the best and the brightest
money managers in the world, and I would be hard pressed to recall
someone who had the command of every global asset class—
currencies, bonds, equities, and of course, commodities—that Renée
has. But it was her enthusiasm, her passion after having done this for
almost three decades, which kept my interest. That, and her propen-
sity to wander off subject a little bit. As someone seeking to find out
as much about my subject as possible, her digressions were more than
okay with me.

Lee Ainslie is a legend in the long/short equity hedge fund universe. Not many people outside of Wall Street know him because he
assiduously maintains a very low profile. In fact, not many people on
Wall Street really know him other than by reputation because he is very
committed to insulating his firm from some of the more intrusive ways
and occasional time-wasting efforts of the sell-side. Humble, he offers
no indication of his incredible success when you meet him. Lee started
his hedge fund career at Tiger Management about the time that I
started covering them as a salesperson at Salomon Brothers, but we
never got to know each other. When Maverick started to emerge as an
important account, I spent more time focusing on them from my perch
in management but always found them somewhat aloof—polite, but
aloof. There was no getting in bed with them like other firms; the
insulated culture was stronger than any other I had seen. I remember
receiving a letter from Lee while I was at Lehman Brothers wherein he
set forth his firm's commission rate, which was an astonishingly low
number, about 75 percent less per share than any other firm with whom
we did business. Fine, we said, we have limited resources and we will
send them elsewhere where we can earn a better return. Fine, he said,

we do our own work anyway. Ultimately, we met somewhere in the middle and enjoyed a cordial firm-to-firm relationship, but I had never met with Lee until our interview. When I decided to write this book, he was one of the first people I thought of and one of the last I thought would cooperate. I sent a few e-mails but did not receive a response. Unfortunately, this was not unusual and I had long ago hardened myself to rejection, perhaps the only enduring benefit of having been an insurance salesman while I attended law school at night. If you want to have any success selling a product that no one wants, surrender is not an option so I decided to give it one more shot with Lee. A few days later he called me on the way to a company retreat and I gave him my pitch. I mentioned all the people we knew in common and I have no doubt he checked with some of them. He is not one to shirk due diligence. During the hours we spent together he did not once leave the conference table to check on what was an incredibly volatile day in the market. Nor did he take any phone calls when his assistant walked in with various messages except for one occasion when it involved his family, a completely understandable response. I won't give away Lee's chapter in this book, but two things came through to me clearer than anything else: he values the process and the culture of his firm above all other factors.

I had never formally met Don Peebles but had watched a couple of his interviews on CNBC. I was impressed with his view on the economy, politics, and real estate investing, his power alley. I got to thinking about how investing in real estate is similar to other investments and concluded that all the same qualities are involved, albeit with different emphasis. What particularly attracted me to Don was that he had an amazing life story and ascent to success. As with women, African Americans are a minority that is under-represented on Wall Street and in finance. With Don being one of the wealthiest African Americans in this country, I thought he would be a tremendous role model for all minorities, but that was too narrow a view. He is a role model for anyone striving for success. I have to admit that I was very surprised that not once did he mention any possible disadvantage he had faced growing up due to race. I felt compelled to raise the question because it did not seem that his story could be complete without discussing this topic. He definitively said it was never a problem, never an issue. I believe his perception is directly attributable to his and his family's strength and determination to reach higher. Don grew up a person of privilege, not the type of privilege that money can bestow, but rather the privilege of being influenced by an entire family that was motivated to achieve. Capitalism is such a part of his DNA that he passed the gene down to his son. He related a story about how his son preferred to return to Florida after they uprooted to New York. Don explained that there is opportunity to become wealthy in Florida, but that you could make billions in New York. The son still wanted out and Don confessed to extreme disappointment. However, his son eventually came around and began on his path, making Don an extremely happy and proud parent. Don's focus on continuing to build his fortune while extending his vision is impressive. A no-excuses guy, he appears to always be looking forward to the next, better opportunity. He is incredibly driven.

I was extremely impressed with Jim Chanos but I admit to being swayed by the fact that he admitted to reading my first book and there it sat, on the bookshelf in his conference room. Being a dedicated short seller, I guess a book about people screwing up (he is usually on the other side of those missteps) is subject matter he could not resist. One of the most diligent investors there is, he makes his living tearing apart balance sheets, seeing the pop when everyone else sees the balloon, ignoring consensus to form his own views. And it is a good thing he has that demeanor because everyone hates short sellers except for their investors. He has testified in front of Congress multiple times and has never had a problem calling governments to task, publicly and loudly, for their missteps and arrogance. China is the current target of his suspicions.

Chuck Royce is also regarded as a pioneer in his chosen investment style: small capitalization stocks. I was shown into his office and he walked over to shake my hand. Where are the shoes, Chuck? Quietly intense, after five o'clock he unwinds. The bow tie comes undone, the top button opens, and he seems to deflate into the chair. Research reports cover virtually every surface in his office. The man loves what he does, and he will do it forever. I started the conversation with small talk and then apologized for taking his time that way. He told me to go on, that this was the only time of day he got to have a real conversation. What a nice guy. He did not show an ounce of stress, but did seem a bit tired. Maybe it was because the market was down more than 2 percent that day, a large drop, and he was busy seeing opportunity and putting money to work.

Tying the Common Threads Together—The Portrait of the Perfect Investor

So what are the common threads running through each of these personalities? What makes them so successful at what they do? And is it possible for someone to replicate these traits and processes with the goal of becoming a better investor? The obviousness of all this makes it almost too simplistic to catalog but, never one to pass up a fat pitch, I am going to proceed with a numbered list.

1. No emotion. Not one of the successful investors I know, and I know many in addition to those chronicled herein, expresses any emotion about the markets. Cool, calm, and levelheaded, they are confident in their strategy and process. In fact, they see the bright side of dislocation—opportunity. They do not get caught up in euphoria and chase stocks or markets, nor do they sell at bottoms because they panicked or were taken by surprise.

2. No ego. There are many big egos in this business and I have seen ego destroy a fund more often than I have seen it work in its favor. No one in this book had any evidence of ego. Self-confidence, yes, but ego, no. They all recognize that they can be wrong at times.

3. Long-term investors. Who really makes money actively trading? Not these people; they have too much money to whip around effectively. And, they profess to not being smart enough to trade the market. Very, very few traders are smart—or lucky—enough to consistently make money trading in and out of positions, particularly with the way the markets have evolved. It takes time for an investment thesis to mature, particularly if you are a value investor and usually early to a story.

4. Discipline. Disciplined risk management and a disciplined investment strategy that they never veer from, ever. Style drift is one of the most popular ways to lose money.

5. Thorough research process. They all have it: the real estate investors, the equity investors, the commodity investors. Diligent, thorough, and disciplined (that word again). They do not buy anything they don't know and will not even look at what does not fit into their style.

6. Passion and work ethic. With unseen opponents and unexpected pitfalls, investing is too tough an endeavor to pursue unless you have passion. Despite the length of time they have been investing and the long days they still put in and the incredible wealth they have all built, they all work extremely hard. Taubman has stepped away from the day-to-day of the company he founded, although he is still the largest shareholder. Instead he has channeled his work ethic to other pursuits, charitable pursuits, working just as hard to find a cure for cancer as he did to build malls and wealth through investments.

7. Drive. They all want to be the best and devote whatever effort it takes to get there. They all have enough money, so wealth is not the motivator except for what it can do for their families and philanthropically. Moreover, it is the challenge of doing well against the markets, of figuring them out and coming out ahead; of being engaged and having a focus.

Drive. Passion. Process. Equanimity. Discipline. Humility. These are the commonalities between all those profiled in this book and the qualities that make for a great—and legendary—investor.

Chapter 2

Follow the Money

The Ugly Reality of Whale Watching

Whale watching—that is, following well-known investors—
is a favorite pastime on Wall Street. The media love
reporting on the latest purchase or sale by Warren Buffett
or Carl Icahn or Steve Cohen. There are expensive newsletters and
data services dedicated to this sport, and no doubt some people have
earned back their subscription fees by mimicking the moves of "legendary" investors. But I contend that blindly following anyone into
a *single* trade is a fool's errand and there are many reasons to support
this conclusion. For one thing, no investor, no matter how legendary,
has a perfect record, and you just might find yourself following a
legend right over a cliff. It is also the case that legendary investors
may have very different investment objectives from yours. For
example, what if the legendary investor is looking long term—happy
and able to be in a position for decades, as Buffett is,[1] while you are

seeking short-term profits? Buffett can wait out a losing position or absorb it as need be, but you, on the other hand, likely do not have the same resources. These can be hard lessons. At least, I found them to be so.

My Wall Street career began on the equity trading desk at Oppenheimer & Co. in what could now be defined as the dark ages of technology. E-mail was more of a novelty than a default communication mode; the Internet was still a twinkle in Al Gore's eye (wink, wink), and High Frequency Trading (HFT) was defined as calling the floor broker and yelling at him in a shrill voice. As the newbie, my job was to hit the lights—trading desk parlance for answering the phone. (With hundreds of incoming calls and a large number of traders, there are no *ringing* phones on a trading desk.) Boredom quickly set in, so I surveyed the cavernous room and determined that my future was in research sales, communicating investment ideas to experienced hedge fund and mutual fund managers. Telling a story, relating an investment case, and debating a much more seasoned investor than myself about the merits of a particular stock was a challenge that I enjoyed; it was far more interesting to me than shopping buy and sell orders on a laundry list of stocks.

So one day, as I sat on the trading desk answering incoming client calls and passing them on to the traders—I hadn't picked up any accounts yet, and since Oppenheimer was a commission shop, it was unlikely anyone would willingly pass any on to me—I decided that having mastered sales trading, I would now try my hand at research sales. I picked up my meager belongings, a pen, a pad, and a book of stock symbols, and moved a few rows back into an open seat on the research sales desk. My boss was a player coach, covering accounts while managing the department, and he was too busy to notice that the most junior person in the room had relocated. A number of days went by before I informed him of my career decision, which was much more important to me than to him. Nonetheless, he would ultimately evolve into one of my favorite colleagues of all time.

It took another few weeks for me to receive my first accounts. This occurred when the saleswoman behind me resigned, complaining that she couldn't "make any money at this place with these accounts," and literally handed me her black loose-leaf binder containing a list of investment managers, banks, and insurance companies she had been assigned to cover. The first thing I noticed was how obediently each page stayed captive to the three metal rings affixed to the binding, not one sheet torn away from its anchor. It didn't take long for me to free them from their bondage. After all, they are supposed to be loose; it's not a tight-leaf binder. On every page was a typed-out contact list for each account the now departed salesperson had covered. No fancy customer relationship management system or electronic database; hell, we didn't even have desktop PCs, only a shared Quotron, the now-ancient system for quoting stock prices that at the time was the standard for market data. I marched into my boss's office, held the binder in front of me, and asked to begin my sales career. "Sure," came the response after a moment's deliberation as a smile formed on his face. "Not what I had in mind for you, but have at it." The something else he had in mind was allowing me to be consumed by boredom while the traders lodged bets on how many times my head would hit the desk as I nodded off while working my way through one dry research report after another. No thanks.

So off I went, energized, calling my new accounts, introducing myself, and finding out as much as possible about every client's particular investment style. It was easy to get through to my new clients; most were small players on Wall Street who didn't get called all that much. At the time, Oppenheimer—OPCO, as it was known— was a small firm compared to Goldman Sachs, Merrill Lynch, and Morgan Stanley, the behemoths then and now, but it did have an excellent research product and a strong core group of analysts. And precisely because this was during the relative dark ages of technology, e-mail and voicemail had not yet became barriers to forming solid relationships and engaging in productive dialogue. In fact, the biggest barrier I faced to becoming a master of the universe was the population of my universe—widow and orphan custodians who did not trade much and rarely ventured away from such blue-chip companies as Coca-Cola and Procter & Gamble. The other barrier was that few had ever done business with Oppenheimer. But I was perhaps too ignorant to be deterred, so I soldiered on, synthesizing and sometimes taking the other side of my analysts' recommendations extolling the virtues of certain companies I deemed to be solid investments.

I began to get traction and turned out to be pretty damn good at stock picking; I was on my way to becoming a top salesperson. In short order, I was given more accounts, accounts that had potential to increase their level of business but were nascent at the time. Unlike the bulk of my account package, composed of clients who were primarily concerned with not making a mistake, these new accounts were more focused on generating returns; they were willing to look at companies that weren't completely correlated to the market indices. They listened to my recommendations, "calls" in the vernacular, but waited weeks, sometimes months, to go along, often keeping track of what I had suggested. Once I earned their trust, I did very well. Oppenheimer's profile was also helpful since the firm followed a large number of companies that were not mainstream thus allowing me to further differentiate myself from salespeople at other firms. Perhaps most helpful of all, it was a bull market. Anyway, I was making money for all my accounts. Well, almost all of them. And herein is the story.

Let's call the account DG Partners. I got along great with them except for one thing: We just never seemed to click at what mattered most—making money. I would recommend a number of stocks for them to buy or short, but DG had an incredible knack for picking the one idea that didn't work out. It started with the first share they bought as it instantaneously went against them, and kept going lower from there. If I suggested a buy idea, the stock would undoubtedly collapse like a balsam step stool under an NFL lineman; a call to short a stock could lead to it hitting the new high list. At one point during our tortured relationship, I suggested that they could make a fortune by going in the opposite direction of my call. After all, consistency is one of the most valuable qualities that a stock-picker can possess, so it shouldn't matter if you're always wrong or always right as long as there is no pretense about the direction. Admittedly, I am embellishing the facts because DG never hung around long enough to lose much, not to mention let an idea play out. They moved in and out of the market very quickly, scalping nickels and dimes while passing up dollars. But the point is that they had an uncanny ability to ignore all my winners, opting instead for the dogs. We liked one another so we continually talked it out, trying to find out why we didn't click.

> "No one can be right all the time," I said defensively.
> "We're not asking for all the time, we're just asking for one time," was the not unreasonable reply.
> "It's just as much your fault as mine. My other accounts don't seem to have the same issue."
> "So why are you giving them the good stuff and us the junk?"
> "That's not the case. I'm making the same call to them as I am to you, but there are two major differences. First, the other trading accounts fire a shotgun at my ideas whereas you guys use a rifle, trying to pick the one idea that will work, that seems the most attractive. I'm just not that good—no one is, at least not within the short time frame that you're going to be holding the stock. Most of the other accounts give the idea some time to work out.
> "I appreciate your confidence in me," I added, clearly tongue in cheek, "but timing of the buy and sell is going to have to be your responsibility since I'll never be as quick as you guys. I'll stick to fundamentals."

No one, not Warren Buffett, not anyone, is so good that they have anywhere near a perfect track record picking stocks. I remember Steve Cohen, one of my ex-bosses and the founder of perhaps the industry's top-performing hedge fund, SAC Capital, saying that the best traders win only 50 to 55 percent of the time. That is the issue right there. Piggybacking on the purchases and/or stock sales of professional investors is an inherently risky strategy, regardless of how successful those individuals have been. The reason is simple: If the best of the best are only right slightly more than half the time, then the average professional is correct in his or her stock selection less than that. But let's be more generous than Steve Cohen by assuming that the hit rate of the best pros is 65 percent. That means that if you pick up the *Wall Street Journal* and read that a very accomplished investor purchased shares in XYZ Company and you decide to follow that investor's lead, you have a better-than-even chance of succeeding. Compared to other endeavors, that isn't terrible. The best hitters in professional baseball sport a batting average close to .300 or 30 percent; the best shooters in the NBA have a field goal average of just over 50 percent; and superstar NFL quarterbacks complete less than 60 percent of their passes, on average. So on this scale professional investors are the true superstars. And while most would tell you they hate to lose any money at all, the truth is they get pretty giddy when their batting average approaches the aforementioned levels. But one investment does not make a profitable portfolio; portfolio construction is so much more critical.

Say that you are willing to accept the odds of following a professional into an investment. So you once again pick up the *Wall Street Journal* and read that some well-known investor who manages billions of dollars—and is worth a billion as well—just filed a Schedule 13D[2] (beneficial ownership report) on a particular company. You immediately log onto your laptop, do a cursory amount of research, and buy a few thousand shares online. *"Good enough for Mr. Billionaire, good enough for me."* Besides, at two to one, the odds are in your favor.

Or say you are scrolling through your news alerts and you discover that David Einhorn, a noted hedge fund manager with a very good track record who made a killing shorting Lehman into the abyss, has just purchased a stake in General Motors (GM). You are also aware that GM is going to release its third-quarter earnings report in a couple of days. Based upon the timing of Einhorn's share purchase, his record for outperformance and reputation for in-depth analysis, you assume that he has a very good feel for the quarter. You decide to follow his lead, buy shares in GM, and look forward to booking a nice gain after the quarterly report. Easy pickings.

The first rule in the investment business is that if it seems too easy, it likely is. And assuming that blindly following large, smart buyers into a stock or other investment will prove to be a winning investment strategy falls into the trouble zone. In fact, you may wind up like my old account, DG Partners, unlucky and on the wrong side of every trade for some of the same reasons. Before buying the equity of a company, a professional considers many factors, including the total number of positions in the portfolio, weighting of each position, risk profile of each position, and the holding period—that is, how long it will take for the investment case of each position to play out. However, none of these factors are decipherable from the Schedule 13D, news stories, or services that capture activity by noteworthy investors or insiders.

Insider Buying: To Follow or Not to Follow

For purposes of this sidebar, let's define *insider* as senior management of a company or a member of the Board of Directors; in other words, someone who is in a position to either influence a company's direction or has significant insight into the execution of the corporate strategy. These individuals are subject to various filing* requirements when they either buy or sell shares, regardless of the size of the transaction, unlike non–insiders who must file when their ownership is equal to or greater than 5 percent of the shares outstanding. As a result of these stringent filing requirements, there are numerous services, offered for free and by subscription, that track this

*The Securities and Exchange Commission offers the following about Form 4: "The information will be used for the primary purpose of disclosing the transactions and holdings of directors, officers, and beneficial owners of registered companies. Information disclosed will be a matter of public record and available for inspection by members of the public."

(Continued)

activity. The subscription services, in particular, offer support for the theory that there is a high correlation between insider activity and the direction of the stock price.

As with most theories on investment strategy, this one should not be taken at face value. For example, senior managers of public companies are receiving a greater portion of their compensation in stock and options, tying them more closely to the financial performance of the company and the share price. Because of this there is significantly more selling activity as those shares vest★ and these insiders seek to diversify their net worth away from the company that also employs them, a prudent strategy. Additionally, Chief Executive Officers are well aware of the reliance some investors place upon insider activity and try to use it to influence the stock price. When I was at Lehman Brothers, Dick Fuld, the CEO, frowned upon his senior management team selling shares because he believed that it would send the wrong message to the market. As a result, very few officers sold any stock. This is likely a directive they deeply regretted following since Lehman would ultimately file for bankruptcy and wipe out its shareholders. Other CEOs will make a token purchase of shares, relative to their net worth, hoping that their purchase makes its way into the news and will then be noticed by potential investors who will follow into the stock. When I review a Form 4 (changes of beneficial ownership of securities) filing by a member of the Board of Directors, a CEO, Chief Financial Officer, or someone of similar seniority, I always look at how many shares are purchased or sold *relative*

★Typically, ownership of the shares or options awarded to an employee phase in over a period of time, usually years. This is the vesting schedule. Employees do not own the shares or options until they vest, and would generally have to be employed by the company on the date they vest to claim ownership.

to their entire holdings and overall compensation. If a very well compensated executive purchases $100,000.00 worth of stock, I basically ignore it as an indicator. Sure, it's nice to see, but hardly a major vote of confidence.

The sale of stock by insiders should not be taken at face value either; I attempt to determine the underlying rationale for any sale before acting upon the information. Since the Internal Revenue Service does not impute ownership of any shares until they are vested, this is when a tax liability arises. Many officers, regardless of wealth, will sell enough shares to cover their taxes. This is a legitimate reason, in my view, as is a sale for the purpose of diversification. Again, everything is dependent upon the totality of the circumstances: years of service, total ownership, compensation, even net worth if discernible.

Perhaps one of the most critical factors in determining the directional value of insider activity is the stock price. If the shares are trading at an all-time low and the executives are selling instead of buying, then I become very concerned. In fact, I may use this as one of the indicators to short the stock.

What it comes down to is this: Company insiders are prohibited from acting on material non-public information. In other words, they cannot either buy or sell shares in their company based upon information that could influence the direction of the stock price before that information is disseminated to the public. Simply put, this would be a violation of insider trading rules. However, transactions by insiders can be an indication of sentiment—how these key employees feel about the business prospects of the company where they work.

Insider activity should have the same value in your investment decisions as whale watching. Use the information as one data point in the research process, placing the appropriate weight on this input as the circumstances dictate.

Of course, the counterargument is that following in the footsteps of a talented investor, particularly when the investor evidences the conviction required to purchase more than 5 percent of a company, can't be a bad thing. There are a few issues with this logic, the first of which is that what may seem like a large position to the average person may in fact be an insignificant holding. For example, the mutual funds run by Fidelity Management are so large that they often have to take filing positions in order for the stock to potentially have an impact on the overall portfolio, the point being that fund managers do different things for different reasons. Without delving deeper than the headline, David Einhorn's rationale for owning GM shares could range from hedging a short position in Ford to wanting to own a proxy for consumer spending, both of which would be very unlikely if you understood his discipline. (This is an extremely important point worth repeating—headlines and insider buying databases do not provide qualitative data.) And of course, the other factors in portfolio construction, as noted above, are also at play. Or Einhorn could just have made a bad stock decision; that happens too. Finally, timing is to be considered. Einhorn is a value player, and value players are notoriously early to a situation, often averaging down their cost and sometimes facing years before their thesis plays out.

So how did this real-life example turn out? Not so well initially but the stock has begun to act much better as of this writing. In a quarterly letter written to the investors in his hedge fund, Greenlight Capital, Einhorn discussed his investment in GM. The document found its way to the Internet on November 7, 2011, the same day it was received by investors.

The pertinent part follows:

GM is the largest auto manufacturer in the United States. After the business failed under its legacy high-cost structure during the recession, the U.S. government bailed out the company and took over most of the ownership. Last November, GM completed an IPO of about 30 percent of *its stock at $33 per share. The government continues to own about one-third of the company. After the IPO, the shares initially advanced to almost $40 before retreating. When the shares broke the IPO price, we determined that the shares were attractive, but only purchased a small position, believing that there might be a better opportunity later when the government exited the rest of its stock. Instead, during a weak third quarter where the market punished all cyclical stocks, the shares fell well below the price where we planned to add to our position. We decided that the shares were cheap enough that we were more than fully compensated for the possible overhang of the government's stake, and we established a position at an average price of $25.78 per share.*

GM is being priced by the market as a cyclical company trading at less than 6x this year's earnings. While some may see it as normal to value cyclicals at low multiples of peak earnings, we believe that 2011 is not a peak and, in fact, is below mid-cycle. Prior to the crisis, U.S. auto sales ran between 15 and 19 million units for many years. While sales have bounced from the recession low to about 13 million units, GM is poised to grow earnings from both a return to mid-cycle volumes, which we estimate to be 15 million units, and from a coming major refresh of its North American product portfolio. The market appears focused on GM's "legacy liabilities." However, the new GM does not have pension and healthcare liabilities that are likely to over-run the company. Instead, GM sits with $33 billion of gross cash, which represents nearly its entire current market capitalization. We see potential for GM to begin to return capital to shareholders over the next year. While we are cognizant of the various investment risks that include near-term global economic weakness and the government ownership overhang, we think these concerns are more than priced in at current levels and see significant upside even if the U.S. experiences a very slow "new normal" type of economic recovery. The shares ended the quarter at $20.18 each.

**Greenlight Capital, Q4 Letter,
November 7, 2001**

Einhorn noted that the average cost of his GM shares was $25.78 and that the stock ended the quarter at $20.18—a 20 percent loss to his fund. However, the price did recover to $24.01 on the day the news media reported on the contents of the letter, slightly outperforming the market. Fast-forward two days to Thursday, November 9, 2011, when GM issued its much anticipated earnings report. The company disappointed investors, traders, and Einhorn followers, and the shares traded down more than 8 percent, resulting in a decline of over $2.5 billion in market capitalization. The stock price, again as of this writing, has since recovered to $25.20. I guarantee that Einhorn wasn't sitting in his office cursing his bad luck but, instead, maintained a stoic commitment to his successful strategy of being a long-term investor. However, I would doubt that the casual investor who followed Greenlight into the stock was as unshaken in their commitment.

What happened? Wasn't Einhorn supremely confident in the outlook for GM as evidenced by his highlighting it in his quarterly letter? Wasn't it a great opportunity for investors to step in and buy the stock at a discount to what a very successful hedge fund manager paid? Yes and yes, but here's the rub: Einhorn takes a very long-term view on stocks, and while he does not want to see any period of underperformance, he is patient; he knows that there will be peaks and valleys along the way as his investment case plays out, so it is too early to make any determination on the ultimate impact GM will have on the performance of his fund. I regard David Einhorn as a brilliant investor, and there is nothing written here that could not also be said about so many other great investors. The overriding issue is that no one has a perfect track record even though his investment in GM may not be one that ultimately resides in the loss column.

Now, in full disclosure, I would be more supportive of someone following Einhorn into GM[3] given that he disclosed his rationale than I would be if that person were just reacting to a headline reporting his fund's ownership in the stock. But I would caution about looking for a quick trade since, as he also noted, his holding period is years, not days, weeks, or months.

Here is another point to consider. The letter mentioned that Greenlight Capital had exited a number of positions in the quarter, all profitable, one flat. What if those stocks had precipitously declined after their exit, and what if one of them happened to be a stock that you had purchased upon hearing that Einhorn was involved? Since none were filing positions, there would not be any way to act in a timely manner relative to Einhorn's decision. As easy as it may be to follow someone into a stock, it can be more difficult to follow him out.

Sometimes it is challenging not to get caught up in the hype surrounding a celebrity investor. Research In Motion Limited (NASDAQ: RIMM), the manufacturer of the Blackberry smartphone, has lost significant market share to Google's Android operating system and the iPhone, resulting in a decline of near 80 percent in its share price in 2011 alone. Despite deteriorating fundamentals, the company continues to be an intriguing investment to some people, no doubt because of familiarity with the product. However, these attempts at catching a falling knife have all ended in losses from the peak price of $70.54 a share in February to the bottom set in December 2011 of $16.00.[4] Taking the market by surprise in November, one of the legendary hedge fund managers mentioned in *The Billion Dollar Mistake* was found to have purchased shares in the company when he released the holdings of his portfolio. This caused a 10 percent spike in the share price as soon as the news hit the tape. I was on television on CNBC that day, and I cautioned that the position size was small relative to the overall size of the portfolio, and that if this investor, whom I knew very well, really had confidence in the stock's potential, he would have owned at least five times the amount that was reported, but that did not seem to matter to those snapping up shares. That evening, I sent an e-mail asking my friend why he had bought Research In Motion, and he responded that it was an extremely small position, so insignificant, in fact, that it was put on by his analyst and, while he did have a conversation with one of the co-chief executive officers at Research In Motion, the recommendation by the analyst did not have to go through the thorough investment policy process required of more meaningful investments. Basically, it was an odd lot, a vote of confidence for someone who worked at his firm. He also mentioned that in his 40 years in the business, no other position had elicited so much attention. This is not to say that this particular manager ever goes into a stock with the expectation of losing money—he guards his capital more zealously than anyone I know—but the approximately $25 million position was well within his risk appetite for speculative bets. The point of this is that while the position was basically insignificant to the professional investor, it likely was significant to those who followed his purchase. They should have followed his rationale and process instead but, and here's the rub, they had no way of knowing what he was thinking. However, if they had performed just a little more due diligence they could have done the math[5] and perhaps saved themselves some aggravation and money, at least in the short term. Postscript: After trading up on the news of the hedge fund's involvement, the stock price hit a new low as the company once again disappointed investors with more bad news, although the story is far from over.

There is an old Chinese proverb that goes something like this: *Give a man a fish and you feed him for a day. Teach a man to fish and you feed him for a lifetime.*

And that is the point of *The Big Win*. This book profiles legendary investors, all of whom are extremely successful, spectacularly wealthy, and very disciplined in how they look at and react to opportunities. Each chapter concludes with an example of a very profitable investment—in the cases of Jim Chanos and Jim Rogers, investment theses that are still playing out as I write. You can go along with them if you like; there is more than enough information on these pages to get you started. The true value of these case studies, however, is in understanding each investor's methods, not standing in awe of their results. Mimicking an investment decision of a smart investor will undoubtedly yield results but not always what was envisioned, despite the odds favoring a positive outcome. The DG syndrome is always lurking in the background.

But understand how a legendary investor thinks, the tenets upon which his or her investment style is based—what the investor looks for in commodities, stocks or bonds or real estate—and you can develop your own profitable strategy that can be applied to all types of investments. Importantly, understand the risk profile of these investors—when they admit to themselves they are wrong, or how they protect their downside when entering into an investment; preservation of capital is by far the most critical factor in any investment strategy. Possessing this knowledge is so much more valuable than whale watching and then blindly following the legendary investor into a trade.

Each *big win* in this book offers a lesson that can be an effective tool for taking greater advantage of the information on what successful investors are buying and selling; the big wins illustrate a tried-and-true process for independently assessing opportunity.

Understand the process, the means to the end. That is what is important, and that is how you can build a repeatable process to generate a positive return over the long term.

Notes

1. Most hedge fund and mutual fund managers have holding periods that fall far short of Warren Buffett's.
2. A Schedule 13D must be filed with the Securities and Exchange Commission within 10 days of a person or group acquiring 5 percent or more of a company's shares with the possible intention of influencing the company. There are other Form 13 filings: 13F is a quarterly report that discloses the stocks held by an institutional investment manager; 13G is a shorter form than the 13D and is used by passive investors. Given issues with liquidity—getting in and out of a sizeable position—and the cost of filing, very few institutional investors will buy enough shares for a "trade" that will require a Section 13 filing.

3. As of this writing, the author has a position in GM shares. Einhorn's analysis made sense and led me to perform my own analysis which included a constructive view on the US economy, a necessity in my view for owning a cyclical company. Consistent with all discussions on stocks in this book, this is not a recommendation to purchase GM shares.

4. As of this writing the stock has rebounded to $17.31, due in part to an upward move in the broader market and continued rumors that the company will be acquired. Owning a stock solely because it is a rumored acquisition target rarely yields positive results.

5. Do the math: A quick search on the Internet would have revealed that the total value of the portfolio referenced in the news reports was about $5 billion, meaning that the fund's position in Research In Motion was approximately one-half of 1 percent of all assets. The same filing that revealed the RIMM position also showed significantly larger portfolio positions, some exceeding 4 percent, indicating RIMM was a lower confidence holding.

Chapter 3

The Glass Ceiling of Performance

Renée Haugerud

R enée Haugerud is a different kind of investor.

It is not just the stellar performance generated over the 14-year life of her hedge fund management firm, Galtere Ltd.—performance marked by only one down year—that draws one to this conclusion.[1] And it is not just because she is a woman in a business still dominated by men. In fact, Haugerud's Galtere Ltd. is one of the largest woman-owned-and-operated funds in the testosterone-fueled hedge fund management industry, and Haugerud, an avowed feminist (although she dislikes the word), is a proud exemplar and champion of what she sees as women's natural affinity for trading. Indeed, to encourage more women to go into the business, Haugerud and her husband have endowed a center at the University of Tennessee in Chattanooga that teaches finance from a woman's perspective and that aims to demonstrate, as 85 Broad's CEO Janet Hanson puts it, that "women are great traders."

What really makes Renée Haugerud a different kind of investor is the perspective that informs her approach to the science and art of trading. It is a perspective shaped by her background in trading "just about every kind of commodity there is" and in her long and deep experience as a grain merchant. "I look at everything as a silo," says Haugerud. "Is it in surplus or deficit, what is the global macro supply and demand, and what do I think will happen as a result? Then I see if there's a trade to be made."

Puts and Calls and Corn

This perspective dates, literally, to Haugerud's childhood in the town of Preston, Minnesota—population 1,200. Her father was the sheriff of Fillmore County, and the Haugeruds shared their home with the county jail. Offenders, ranging from the town drunk to convicted murderers, were literally just down the hall; the circumstances alone taught the young Renée something about risk and imbued her with the sense that "things are not always what they seem."

Neil Haugerud, Renée's father, was a bright and active fellow. His career and interests were eclectic, ultimately including published author,[2] state legislator, farmer, and amateur pilot. It was the combination of the latter two endeavors that would have the most impact on forming Renée's career path. During a father-daughter flight over the cornfields she had an epiphany of sorts, at least as much of an epiphany as a five-year-old can muster. After checking out his own fields that lay just outside of town, Haugerud kept flying across the state line to survey cornfields in Iowa. "Why are we looking at these fields?" young Renée wanted to know. "We don't own these."

"No," explained her father, "but there's this thing called the futures exchange. It makes it possible," as he goes on to spell out in some detail, "to enter into a contract for a transaction at a later date, so it is important to gather as much information as possible about all the crops."

"You mean," asked Renée, "that you can sell this guy's corn without owning it?"

"That's pretty much it," her father replied. The idea was *phenomenal* to Renée Haugerud. It ignited her mind and lit a fire that nothing has managed to extinguish. A young child picks up a hammer and an observer offers, "He'll be a carpenter when he grows up." Should a kindergartener pull a stalk of corn from the ground, one may offer, "I bet she'll be a farmer." However, the words, "Looks like we have a budding commodity trader on our hands" have likely never been uttered. The fact that such a young mind was able to grasp so complicated a concept was likely testimony to both her father's storytelling ability and his daughter's intelligence and seemingly innate ability to grasp all things relating to commodities. In any event, the figurative seeds were planted for what would be a very successful career.

Meanwhile, Renée enjoyed a resolutely normal Midwestern childhood—as normal as you can have when your living quarters share the same building as the county jail. When the time came for college she indulged her love of the outdoors and went off to the University of Montana at Missoula to major in forestry. She eschewed graduate business school, feeling that an MBA might muddy her raw, out-of-the-box thinking in the same way that an adventurous chef might forego cooking school. Besides, she already had real-life exposure to what a graduate degree might have provided: Her father had taught her the basics of puts and calls, and she had followed the exchanges since she was a kid.

Never a slacker, when faced with time to fill between her December graduation and her start date as a staffer on the Minnesota legislature's Natural Resources Committee, she set out to find work. With a natural curiosity for all things business, Haugerud wanted to use this time to gain exposure to different parts of the world of commerce. Administrative roles were all that were available to a young woman coming out of college, but she would not be the first, or the last, female whose exposure to corporate America came through office work—filing, answering phones, and of course making coffee for the men. Rather than mark time until June, Haugerud looked upon the temp jobs as a way to see how companies worked. One of her assignments landed her at Cargill, long a fixture on the Minnesota landscape and a mainstay of the state's and the region's economy as an international producer and marketer of food, agricultural, financial, and industrial products and services. Cargill is one of the largest privately owned companies in the world. In addition to its commodity and commodity trading business, it produces a wide variety of consumer products from food to animal health items and pharmaceuticals. It also has a significant business trading energy products and in biofuel manufacturing. It was a company Renée liked from her first day on the job, no doubt testimony to the collegial culture even in the midst of the bustling atmosphere. Besides, who would not be charmed by a company whose president took the time to say hello to a temporary office worker as he passed by her desk?

After a few days of filing, Haugerud asked the person next to her, "What does this company do, anyway?"

"They trade things."

"And how does one get to do that?" Haugerud wanted to know next.

"You need to be a merchant."

If her father's description of futures trading had been a revelation, this simple exchange beside the file cabinet struck Haugerud with a shock of recognition. Being a merchant trading grain, she quickly understood, was exactly what she wanted to do with her life. It would require an understanding of every kind of market, knowledge of agriculture, currencies, economics, weather, and human beings, and it would demand that she travel. Nothing could be better. Lacking the officially stated qualifications of being interviewed on a pre-approved university campus for the grain merchant's job,

Haugerud pestered Cargill's Human Resources Department for six months until she was granted an interview, during which she thoroughly convinced her interviewers that they should hire her. "I wanted to be a grain trader so bad I could taste it," says Haugerud. It came through in her presentation. Cargill management yielded on the qualifications, and Haugerud began a 13-year stint at the venerable company, starting with an assignment as a grain originator in Kansas City.

Then and now, Cargill is a large organization. Privately held, it generated more than $100 billion in revenues in 2010, the last year for which figures were available as this book went to press. These revenues were derived from products as diverse as natural gas, Crisco cooking oil, Purina dog food, and of course, most importantly, trading in commodities. As an almost necessary adjunct to their core business, Cargill actively trades in the commodities and securities markets. While some of this activity is to hedge their costs, it is also pursued for profit. In fact, some regard Cargill as a gargantuan hedge fund, and there is significant practical support for that view. What better place to learn how to trade than a company that is *the market* for virtually all soft commodities?

A Feel for Trading

It is easy to see why rules about qualifications and a traditional preference for men in the grain merchant ranks gave way to Renée Haugerud's persistence and passion. Blonde, blue-eyed, the picture of Midwestern wholesomeness, Haugerud is very much a body in motion. In the high-design Galtere Ltd. offices she occupies in the storied Scribner Building on New York's Fifth Avenue, where legendary editor Maxwell Perkins worked with F. Scott Fitzgerald, Ernest Hemingway, and Thomas Wolfe, Haugerud tells her story in the inherited flat accent of the heartland but with the speed of the New Yorker she has become. It is this blending of her roots in the farm belt with her learned expertise as a trader that forms the basis for her success.

"If you don't ask, it will never happen," she says, and it might be the mantra of her entire career, whether referring to a job, raising money, or the recognition she so richly deserves and has attained. She spent two years in origination, the area of Cargill that essentially prepares the structure for a trade, before being named a trader, working a small program in corn. One day, she got a call from someone asking for a bid on sunflower seeds—called "sunnies." As it turned out, no one in the regional office was trading sunnies nor did they want to; sunnies had not been a big enough market for anyone to have an interest. However, this caller had three barges of sunnies on the river, and Haugerud knew that if priced right they could make some good money. Until that phone call, Haugerud had no experience in trading sunnies, but consistent with a career in which she has capitalized on opportunities that others have not seen, she asked for and was granted the authority to run her own sunnies desk within Cargill.

Her first order, to buy those three barges of sunnies at the right price, was an eye-opener that confirmed her always-ask mantra and gave her a crash course in negotiation. Looking to eventually sell sunnies both domestically and to Mexico, Haugerud sought to negotiate rail shipping rates that were far below the usual levels in order to insure that the trade was profitable. "It will never happen," she was told. Unwilling to let the first word be the final word, she coaxed her transportation colleague to negotiate with the railroads for a short-term freight contract at her price. She then had to convince her colleagues in the elevator storage division at Cargill to allocate space for her newly purchased sunnies. They finally agreed, and her trade would eventually achieve profit margins significantly higher than usual. Haugerud was on her way: "I never looked back—and I have loved every single minute of it."

The Cargill career fleshed out the trading curriculum as perhaps no other experience could have. Haugerud mastered currency trading at the company's foreign exchange desk in Geneva, Switzerland. She added expertise in fixed income with a stint back home in Minneapolis, then moved about as far away from home as possible when she was named to manage the branch financial markets office in Melbourne, Australia. There, she oversaw trading portfolios in currencies, fixed income, and equities while also being responsible for accounting and all the other aspects of operating a business within a country office.

She did not just learn how to execute trades; she was so good that she could see inside of them. She knew that her market and asset class analysis differed from that of the majority of investors, and that she had an instinctive feel for identifying a trading opportunity; she could sense a situation beginning to vibrate at a certain pitch that told her there was a trade to be made. Across the continents and through the years, Haugerud thought long and hard about the process of trading and about her own vision of it, and when she came home to Cargill headquarters, she pitched management a business plan for a proprietary risk-taking trading desk based on her ideas and on the technical price analysis model she herself had devised. Management green-lighted the plan and Haugerud formed the Structural Trading Department, operating it as an internal macro hedge fund.

But even having her own in-house fund did not dampen the passion to capitalize on her strategy in her own way, especially since Haugerud was aware that, despite her affection for and gratitude to Cargill, she was "the wrong gender, the wrong political persuasion, and very opinionated." Hedge fund managers tend to be extremely independent, a trait born of necessity; consensus thinking rarely leads to maximizing the return on an investment. And with this independence comes a personality that ultimately needs to own the entire process. So in 1997, Haugerud came to New York and founded Galtere Ltd., determined to give free rein to her vision and to put to work the trading strategies and analytical tools she had developed over the years.

It was not an easy ramp. Haugerud put everything she had into getting Galtere off the ground, but she never wavered in her conviction or her strategy. Initial efforts at raising capital proved difficult and funding the enterprise was extremely challenging. Successful traders understand that they are often early to the game, and this can result in a lag between their recognition of value and the moment when the perception of others catches up. By day, her loft was an office, by night a bedroom, as she sought to keep costs down and dedication high. Ultimately, there was a moment of truth when her life savings were nearly depleted, not from poor investments, but from overhead. She decided that a visit with her former colleagues at Cargill was in order, not to relive her past trading accomplishments, but with a proposition to include them in her new venture. Benefitting from a legacy of strong relationships and perhaps an even stronger record of profits, her former boss decided to make a sizeable investment in Galtere. This seal of approval from Cargill was what potential investors needed to see. It provided enough critical mass for her to be taken seriously, a revenue stream assuming positive investment returns, and a strong vote of confidence from a well-respected organization that had the advantage of having worked with her for more than a decade.

Commodities as Mover and Shaker

Commodity-focused global macro investors understand the term to mean a kind of investment strategy applied to a commodities portfolio. Haugerud, as always, sees it differently. In her worldview, just about everything has been commoditized—"not only real assets but currency and even culture"—and therefore, as the leading indicator, commodities "will move the other asset classes." As to global macro, Haugerud disputes the idea that it is a strategy. "It's a base of research incumbent on anyone trading," she says.[3] See Figure 3.1, which spells out Galtere's strategy.

No one would cavil with Haugerud's terminology. Define commodity based global macro trading however you like; she has made

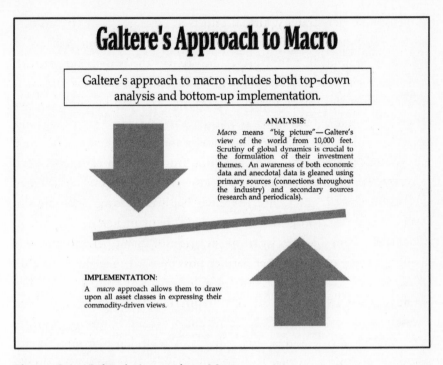

Galtere's Approach to Macro

Galtere's approach to macro includes both top-down analysis and bottom-up implementation.

ANALYSIS:

Macro means "big picture"—Galtere's view of the world from 10,000 feet. Scrutiny of global dynamics is crucial to the formulation of their investment themes. An awareness of both economic data and anecdotal data is gleaned using primary sources (connections throughout the industry) and secondary sources (research and periodicals).

IMPLEMENTATION:

A *macro* approach allows them to draw upon all asset classes in expressing their commodity-driven views.

Figure 3.1   Galtere's Approach to Macro
SOURCE: Information provided by Galtere Ltd., November 2011.

a lot of money doing it, and her approach, while predictably unconventional, is as methodical and inventive as the woman herself.

First the big picture, then the theme, then the trade. Figures 3.2 and 3.3 chart the process.

That is the Haugerud approach in a nutshell. It is simple, but that is the point. Most investing, she contends, is based on the past; it focuses on asset class or geography and looks back at what happened. The result is to make trades much more complicated than they need to be or ought to be. Haugerud is certain that simple is smart, and her success confirms her conviction.

"I am top-down," she says, "and I always start at the top." The first task is to take the temperature of the market, just as a doctor would take a patient's temperature as a prelude to any diagnosis. In

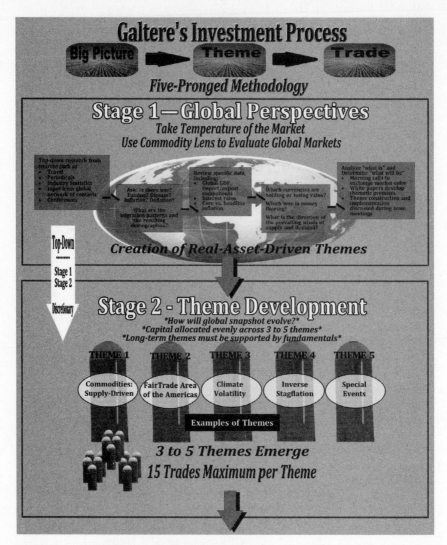

Figure 3.2 Galtere's Investment Process, Stages 1 and 2
SOURCE: Information provided by Galtere Ltd., November, 2011.

the case of the economy of the planet, however, that means measuring the fundamental dynamics that may portend a pattern change or a shift in the way the world works: Is there war somewhere? Is there famine? Disease? Inflation? Deflation? What are the migration patterns among people and the resulting demographics; that is, where are people going to find or create economic value—and what places

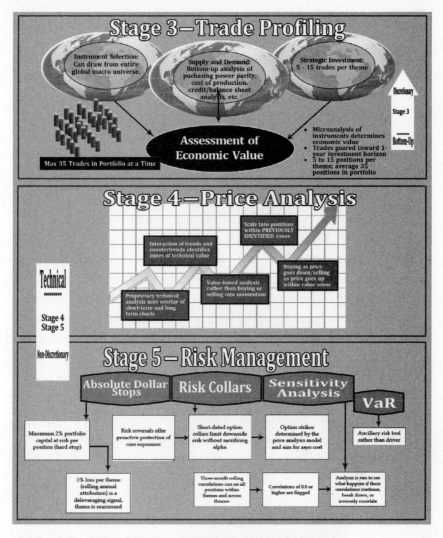

Figure 3.3 Galtere's Investment Process, Stages 3 through 5
SOURCE: Information provided by Galtere Ltd., November, 2011.

are they leaving to do so? Which way is the money flowing, and which currencies are holding or losing value? Importantly, what are the relationships among asset classes—and what is the direction of the prevailing winds of supply and demand?"

The information that emerges from this fundamental analysis leads Haugerud to define from three to five themes—conceptualized like the silos of her grain trading days—each of which will yield no more than 15 trades for a total portfolio containing approximately 35 trades at any one time. To get into the portfolio, a proposed trade must meet two criteria: One, it must be able to produce economic value based on the fundamentals—"I am a value trader, not a momentum trader," says Haugerud; and two, it must fit into one of Haugerud's technical value zones—undervalued if the trade goes long, overvalued to go short.

This wide-angle view gives Haugerud what she believes is a clear edge in evaluation of the fundamentals—namely, it allows her to catch things that others miss. It also offers an advantageous starting point for the next step in the process, which is price analysis modeling to determine what she calls value zones. Basically, the task is to analyze how the dominating global forces may affect commodities prices and how interest rates, currencies, and equities may therefore be impacted. She uses the proprietary technical analysis model she herself devised, based on her grain trading experience, to sift through the big-picture view, drawing bands of undervaluation and overvaluation across the raw data.

Galtere Ltd.'s inverse stagflation theme exemplifies the process Haugerud has put in place. Its starting point, as seen through the wide-screen big-picture lens, is the rising value of commodities coupled with the falling value of paper assets like stocks and bonds. With real interest rates extremely low, money is plentiful while commodities, for which demand is high and rising, are in short supply. This is the simple reality, and it yields a pragmatic proposition for strategic action—namely, that the simultaneous occurrence of inflation and deflation represents a substantive shift from the three-decades-long performance dominance of paper assets over commodities.

That's how long it has been since the world last saw simultaneous inflation and deflation. Paper assets, both stocks and bonds, bottomed in 1982 after a period of stagflation in the mid to late 1970s. The difference was that back then the simultaneous inflation and deflation happened in exactly the opposite way: Commodities prices moved sideways and paper assets soared in value. It took a couple of decades for commodities to recover, and by the time of the 2007 to 2008 global financial crisis, both commodities and paper assets were booming. Since then, however, commodities have continued their rise without a concomitant rise in interest rates, which one usually expects with any kind of inflation, real asset or otherwise. Haugerud contends if you try to sell bonds to hedge against inflation it will not work this time. This time the world is not short of money. She also says that even if interest rates stay low a positive equity market is not assured. Baby boomers are finally starting to shorten duration along with major demographic shifts in wealth and consumption. In her view, "Equities are the most over-invested, over-valued, mismanaged asset class in the world—and everybody is invested in them." Put it all together and you have a sure-fire formula for adjusting your asset allocation—not just in commodities but in currencies and precious metals, all of which are affected.

The real key this time, says Haugerud, is the emerging markets, which are consuming their way to prosperity. As their economies grow, bringing millions out of poverty, the standard diet is changing, demand for food—especially for protein food—is growing, and there is upward pressure on agricultural products and farmland. In fact, as Haugerud sees it, any commodities-rich country will experience a convergence in interest rates, currencies, and equities based on commodities being not solely an asset but also a currency.

Haugerud does not bring any geographic bias to her trading; having had more than 20 mailing addresses she has called "home" during her 30-year career has instilled in her a belief that an open mind is critical to uncovering investable themes, managing risk, and, ultimately, performance. An open mind doesn't mean that strong opinions are not welcome at Galtere. In fact, strong conviction is required. But assumptions driving financial and commodity markets are subject to change without notice, which makes it essential that confidence not rise to the level of obstinacy.

Managing Risk

Commodity cycles are never smooth or easily predicted; there could well be supply shocks, a dearth of inventory. The history of the first decade of the twenty-first century alone tells us that the unexpected, the unforeseen, and the unpredicted happen with stunning regularity. That is why Haugerud has defined a risk management system that is clear, precise, and quite rigorous.

"Risk versus reward is everything," she says, "and Galtere Ltd. will not put on a trade unless we can make about three times what we risk." To keep it simple, Haugerud has established—and follows— strict rules on "what we risk." One rule is that she won't tolerate a loss of more than two percent of the portfolio at any time; she calls it a "hard-coded stop" aimed at protection against potentially extreme events. Another is that risk collars of two-week to two-month options are "mandatory on all full-risk positions"—a kind of insurance policy that Haugerud says helps her sleep at night. In truth, I suspect that her mind never shuts off; a global portfolio rotates through each time zone, with something always trading somewhere, at all times.

The unexpected can happen on both sides of the equation, of course, but for Haugerud, as long as the underlying reasons for a trade are still valid, she stays in—and she is constantly questioning whether the reasons are still valid, another key to her risk management process. As she puts it, she needs "to be right for the right reasons. Even if I'm making money, if the fundamental reasons for being in the trade change, I get out." She did exactly that when she shorted the Hang Seng; the trade was profitable, but Haugerud "closed the theme because I was right for the wrong reasons." She says: "Making money for the wrong reasons means you are rolling the dice, not trading. We are not here to gamble."

The rules her firm follows are very simple and very pragmatic: There are limits imposed on the size of the portfolio, strict criteria for entry into the portfolio, hard-coded rules for staying in or being kicked out. And tough as it sounds, Haugerud "cannot recall an instance where we did not find at least five trades in a given theme that met our valuation criteria." The reason, she believes, is diversity, which she prizes both as the best way to identify successful trades and as a risk management tool in and of itself. She seeks portfolio diversity through diversity of trades, which she tries to ensure by hiring a variety of traders—men and women of diverse backgrounds and cultures. This amalgamation of cultures promotes differing perspectives on each trade that the Galtere team subjects to due diligence. She looks for trading skill—or perhaps the inherent sense for the feel of a trade that she herself possesses—rather than for expertise in particular instruments or geographies or strategic ideas. "The key is to find someone who could make money trading nuts and bolts in a hardware store if she were forced to," says Haugerud—or perhaps by trading the grain waiting on three barges for the merchant who can put together the right buyers at the right price for the right cost of shipping. It is another form of the pragmatic simplicity Renée Haugerud has built into her trading proposition.

Renée Haugerud's Big Win: The Three-Instrument Trade

Haugerud is a facts junkie who loves to peruse statistics to see what broad-brush relationships she might find there. One day in 1993, she was doing just that while reading *The Economist*. Specifically, she was grazing among the figures on that venerable journal's famed back pages, where the editors print what might be called the extremes of the week—highest and lowest rates, strongest and weakest currencies, best and worst stock and commodities exchange figures.

She was checking out which commodities were trading the most-over and the most-under their cost of production, and the figures for gold caught her eye. It had the lowest nominal interest rate and was trading at well above the world's highest cost of production—in fact, at as much as 40 percent above, while her take was that production costs would soon be dropping.

Another figure caught her eye as well: the bonds issued by some of Canada's western provinces. She knew the provinces were rich in commodity resources, and *The Economist* statistics made it clear that the provincial bonds had among the highest nominal interest rates of all developed countries.

What are the relationships among asset classes, and which way are the prevailing winds blowing? Two key questions of the Haugerud temperature-taking process immediately came to the fore, and the answers made it clear to her that she could short gold, the world's most expensive commodity, and thereby fund the purchase of the Canadian provincial bonds at the lowest rate.

To execute the trade, Haugerud borrowed gold, listed at the time at \$410 per ounce, for a rate of less than 1 percent. With what she calls "a bit of leverage," she then used it as the funding currency to buy one-year bonds issued by Saskatchewan, Alberta, and British Columbia at from 9 to 12 percent.

She also looked around for a way to hedge her short gold position further. She wanted something that would hold its value if gold went down and would do even better than gold if it rallied. What would that be? Haugerud began to explore undervalued small-cap mining equities in South Africa, Canada, and Australia that had high margins and production costs of under \$300 per ounce. She found what she was looking for among small-cap mining producers in Australia who took a big loss when bullion lost \$60 and gold fell to \$350—great value, she thought, even if gold kept going down.

"All three legs worked," as Haugerud puts it, and all kept working for a good long while. It was a simple trade, and the returns were good enough to carry that year's performance to her stated goal and beyond.

It should also be noted that Haugerud had never traded in any of the three instruments before. A trade is a trade is a trade.

The Takeaway

Ideas are where you find them, be it from watching the screen and catching dislocations in price, to simple conversations, to the back pages of esteemed publications. But while *The Economist* planted the initial seed for Galtere's triad of ideas, it was only recognizable as a money-making opportunity because of Haugerud's vast experience fleshed out by a strong research effort. Background, intellect, and due diligence provided the confidence to understand the trade, to extend it past a single position in gold, and to stay the course during the ups and downs of the positions. Picking one idea, much less three, is often a greater challenge than most can conquer consistently—particularly in the volatile and sometimes obtuse commodity and currency markets.

Perhaps more important than finding an investment opportunity is being in a position to understand it when you see it. That is why an *open mind* is the primary takeaway from this chapter, because it covers so many important issues for the professional and average investor. Haugerud had been focused on starting her career with the government. Perhaps it was her degree in Forestry that allowed her to see the forest through the trees (apologies for the play on words) during her brief tenure in a clerical position at Cargill and be able to discern the opportunity the company had to offer.

But no one was offering the opportunity, so Haugerud called upon the persistence that would be a critical component in her eventual success and secured an interview, then a position. She did not break new ground as a woman on a Cargill trading desk—there had been a few others—but neither was it an easy get, particularly for someone essentially coming out of the outsourced temp secretary pool.

(Continued)

Luck helped. After breaking through to the trading ranks, it was by sheer chance that she happened to answer the phone when the guy called in with his sunnies. Haugerud saw opportunity where no one else had before. She kept an open mind and would not take no for an answer when told that the rail rates were fixed. By will, charm, and sheer hard work, she persuaded others to have an open mind too—persuaded her boss to allow her to trade sunnies, persuaded the shipping manager to negotiate, and finally persuaded the seller lugging the three barges down the river.

As she continued to keep her mind free from barriers, she spent time trading all asset classes in every time zone where Cargill was active, prying open the minds of others as she became the first woman to run several trading desks: grains, currency, credit, branch offices, and then the Structural Department. It was not an easy journey up the hierarchy, particularly with so many talented traders as colleagues. And certainly it helped that Haugerud's direct supervisor was not influenced by gender. He was not the usual governor regulating the supply of successful women succeeding on Wall Street; instead, he used only P&L, profit and loss, as an assay of talent. It was a performance measure in which Haugerud excelled.

Persistence and an open mind contribute enormously, but do not guarantee Renée's continued success. It is also true that these qualities, while admirable, are insufficient when standing alone so let's add in a few others. Renée believes that gender is another important factor. She contends, in this instance from a position of bias, that, contrary to the usual characterization of women, they generally possess a lack of emotion and ego when it comes to trading and are therefore best at it. Emotional investing is an oxymoron because strong feelings get in the way of objective analysis. It is critically important not to be married to an investment just because the trade has already been put on, falling in love when it goes up and hanging on too long, or letting your ego convince you that you are smarter than the market when the investment thesis heads south. Keeping an open mind—whoops, said it again—is critical at both ends of the spectrum and in between as well, when the trade is not working and keeps soaking up opportunity cost. Not making a decision on a position in your portfolio is a decision made by inaction, so you are either committed to it as something that you would have bought then and there or you should get rid of it.

Seek out different perspectives. If you surround yourself with people who all think alike, talk alike, and come from essentially the same background, it is more difficult to generate a fresh investment idea. Whenever I buy or short a stock, I try to find someone on the opposite side of the trade. Of course, it is always easier to find someone who is long rather than short, but I still try to find a person I respect who can play devil's advocate with me, providing a different perspective. If I am considering an investment in Europe such as shorting the Euro, I want to have a dialogue with informed currency traders who are long and others who are short, preferably adding a European economist into the mix. Only by hearing different and opposing views can an investor work through the rationale for a trade and be confident that it is worth the investment. Haugerud surrounds herself with analysts of diverse nationalities and training—not an onsite resource available to most individual investors. That is where persistence and a strong research ethic enter the picture. Much of what is needed is available on the Internet, and

(Continued)

sophisticated search engines make it easy to uncover multiple perspectives.

Knowing when *not* to have an open mind is another takeaway from this chapter. There should be a compelling thesis underpinning every investment and rigorous monitoring of how it evolves. Great investors judge themselves based upon their ability to discern and profit from their process, regarding luck as an unrepeatable event, not a cornerstone to their success. When a trade goes against you, focus on why; if your investment case is still intact it may be a buying opportunity. But if the adverse result is due to unforeseen events that mitigate your thesis, get out. Conversely, if the investment works out for a different reason than you had foreseen, close out the position since you are now in unknown waters and good luck can become misfortune in the blink of an eye. In short, know why you are there and don't ever find another reason for staying. Fundamentals, not price action alone, are what should control your investment strategy.

A Rare Sighting: The Female Role Model on Wall Street

The Buttonwood Agreement, signed on May 17, 1792 under a buttonwood tree on the site of what is now 68 Wall Street, is credited with being the forerunner of the New York Stock Exchange. Over the next 300 years, a lot would change, but for all the positive strides, something that has remained static is the complexion and gender of the industry; Wall Street is still largely the bastion of white males. I never paid much attention to the lack of women or minorities on the Street—until my daughters were born; then it began to hit home. As

I moved into management, I endeavored to be gender-blind, and the result was that as far as I could tell, I wound up with a desk with more women filling the seats than any other at Lehman Brothers. Perhaps it is a good time to mention that my sales force was ranked number one on Wall Street, besting firms like Goldman Sachs, Morgan Stanley, and Merrill Lynch with their vanilla composition. This success was not good enough for one particular colleague at Lehman, who could not understand why I was paying one of the women on my desk a full year's bonus despite her impending maternity leave. "Where's she going to go if you don't pay her?" this moron wanted to know. "Who's going to hire someone who's pregnant and leaving for three months?" "You have three daughters," I reminded him, my distain evident. "Is that how you want them treated?"

Fast-forward 10 years. My younger daughter is seeking an internship on Wall Street prior to her sophomore year in college. After a number of interviews at different firms, she asks me why there aren't *any* women in senior positions. "That's up to you to change," I offered in return. Being the person that she is, she enthusiastically accepted the challenge (and as a first step secured an internship in Investment Banking, a very rare occurrence for a sophomore). Pleased by her determination, I was also saddened by her dead-on observation and by knowing that her path will not be as easy as it is for those not handicapped by gender or race. This exchange is what prompted me to seek out a woman to include in this book—a role model for my kid and for all the daughters out there. It is a sad commentary in itself that the number of women at the top is so limited that Renée Haugerud, one of the few women to manage a hedge fund of size, was easy to spot. However, it is not her gender that

(Continued)

sets her apart but rather her performance. Since the March 1999 launch of Galtere Ltd. through the first 10 months of 2011, the fund has returned almost 300 percent to its initial investors, generating an average annual return in excess of 11 percent. That is world-class performance replicated by few other funds. In fact, over the same time period, the broadest market measurement, the Standard & Poor's 500 Index, was basically flat.

Earlier in 2011, for the first time in history, women took over as the majority of the workforce in the United States. While their numbers have improved only slightly at the very top of corporate America, they now dominate middle management. Statistics from the U.S. Bureau of Labor show that women now hold more than 50 percent of managerial and professional jobs, such as accounting and banking, and they represent half of all associates in law firms. This is a substantial increase from 1980 when they accounted for a little more than 25 percent of these jobs.[*]

However, the battle for equality has hardly been won as women still make up an almost imperceptible percentage of hedge fund managers, even though their performance has been shown to surpass that of men. In the beginning of 2008, woman oversaw a paltry 3 percent of the then $1.9 trillion invested in hedge funds.[†] The following excerpt from a 2010 study, entitled *Women In Fund Management: A Road Map for Achieving Critical Mass—and Why It Matters,* is very enlightening:

[*]www.theatlantic.com/magazine/archive/2010/07/the-end-ofmen/8135/.
[†]G. Fabrikant, "Corner of Finance Where Women Are Climbing." Retrieved September 17, 2008, as found in www.txwsw.com/pdf/women_fund_mgt.pdf.

Launched in 2007, the HFRX Diversity Index published by Hedge Fund Research, Inc. tracks the (pro forma) performance of hedge fund portfolios managed by women and minorities in its Diversity Universe. The Index, which includes roughly one-half women managers, has returned 8.21 percent on average per year (pro forma) since 2003, compared with 5.98 percent for HFR's broader index (the HFRI Fund Weighted Composite). In the down market of 2008, the difference was dramatically greater: the Diversity Index returned −5.41 percent, compared to −19.03 percent for the broader index. In the first quarter of 2009, as the market struggled back, returns for the Diversity Index were up 2.79 percent, with the broader index returning just 0.38 percent. In an industry driven by performance, this outcome should put to rest the long-held assumption that women are not as good managers as men and validates efforts to seek out the best women–run funds, particularly by institutional investors who have explicit diversity goals.*

Source: The National Council for Research on Women

But performance is apparently not nearly enough to draw more capital to women money managers, as the same study also points out:

In fact, statistics show that gaining access to capital in general is a greater challenge for women than it is for men. For instance, although women currently own nearly a third of all U.S. businesses, female entrepreneurs historically have received a disproportionately low share of available venture capital—as little as 4 percent, according to a Kauffman Foundation study, "Gatekeepers of Venture Growth: The Role and Participation of Women in the Venture Capital Industry.[4]

Source: The National Council for Research on Women

Haugerud and her husband, John "Murph" Murphy, are working to change the perception that causes this phenomenon

*www.txwsw.com/pdf/women_fund_mgt.pdf.

(Continued)

to persist and are leading not just by example but also in deed. They recently donated $2 million to the University of Tennessee at Chattanooga, three-quarters of which will be allocated to develop a program that "will offer women the foundation for a successful career in finance and business and ultimately, cultivate essential life skills." A million and a half dollars to get the ball rolling on providing opportunity for women traders will hopefully provide Haugerud with her biggest return on investment yet.

Notes

1. The full fund performance of Galtere Ltd. suffered only one negative return year, 2008, when it was down 1.8 percent. This was stellar performance, considering that the average hedge fund lost 16 percent of capital and the average mutual fund declined by 37 percent in line with the S&P 500, the common benchmark of performance.
2. Neil Haugerud, *Jailhouse Stories, Memories of A Small Town Sheriff* (Minneapolis: University of Minnesota Press, 1999).
3. It is well worth noting that a recurring theme in every chapter of this book is that each investor follows a disciplined research process.
4. "Gatekeepers of Venture Growth: The Role and Participation of Women in the Venture Capital Industry" (Kansas City, MO: Kauffman Foundation, 2004).

Chapter 4

The Boom Goes Bust

James S. Chanos

One can imagine Marco Polo, back in the thirteenth century, uttering the prescient phrase, "China is the future." In the twenty-first century, it has become the nearly universal mantra repeated by savvy investors and the general public, uttered with increasing frequency and conviction. Certainly in the first decade of this century, had you asked just about anyone in the United States or western Europe, especially if they were sitting around a conference table at a forum on global economics, where to put your money for future growth, that is what they would have answered: China. China was seen as the world's new economic power, replacing the West. It was where the new wealth would be made.

To some, this made China the world's savior, since China was the fastest growing economy on earth by galloping leaps and bounds and, as of this writing, remains the second largest economy on the planet. It seemed well positioned to do the heavy lifting that would eventually haul the rest of the world up and out of global recession. If the once-dominant economic powers of the West were to decline a bit in the rankings as a result, that was okay by them. Everyone has a price, and increasing prosperity is never a bad price to pay.

To others, the China phenomenon seemed scary. They viewed China's growth as the key competitive threat to Western hegemony, and particularly to U.S. hegemony, not just economically but in every other sphere—political, cultural, even military. Some of these folks— like bombastic billionaire Donald Trump—saw the competition with China as a war, to be fought on every front. For others—most notably for mega-investor Jim Rogers (who will be featured in Chapter 8), China was the opportunity he urged his children to embrace. It was not just talk on Rogers's part. He sold all his U.S. assets and moved his family lock, stock, and barrel to Singapore to enable his daughters to embrace the opportunity *now*—his personal commitment to giving them a stake in the kind of future every parent wishes for his or her children.

And so it went. Among the talking heads on the financial chat shows, in newspapers and popular publications, even as a punch line among late-night comics, just about everyone concurred: China's economy was the one on an upward spiral, and the baton of economic power would soon be passed from west to east. Pretty soon now, we would all be working for the Chinese. This became the conventional wisdom, and it was accepted and advanced with virtual unanimity.[1] Keep this thought in mind for now—there will be more on China later; it isn't going away.

There was the odd naysayer, however. A handful of doubters. A few analysts skeptical of the conclusions being drawn so blithely from the known facts about China's economic activity. One of the most prominent among them was Jim Chanos, the short seller. But then, saying nay is Chanos's stock in trade; a disinclination to accept conventional wisdom without questioning it up, down, and sideways, comes naturally. It is what short sellers do—they bet against a stock with the aim of profiting from its falling price—and Chanos runs the biggest short selling fund in the business, Kynikos Associates.

A Fan of the Facts

Thinking about the markets comes naturally to him as well. As a boy in Milwaukee, Jim Chanos heard repeatedly from his father that "you'll never get rich working for somebody else." Instead, he was told, you must run your own enterprise or get rich through the markets. Jim would eventually do both.

He started by reading about the markets—not unusual, except that Chanos was in the third grade at the time. Markets and money were a frequent topic of conversation in the Chanos household—Chanos's father owned a chain of dry-cleaning stores, and his mother worked in a steel company's administrative office. At Yale, where he eventually majored in economics, he wrote his senior thesis on presidential election cycles, monetary policy, and stock market returns. Chanos loved researching.

Investing was certainly the business he wanted to be in, but Chanos had no interest in going to New York after Yale. Instead, upon graduating in 1980, he sent out resumes to firms in Chicago and took an analyst position offered by what had just become, via merger, Blythe Eastman Paine Webber. The merger joined two white-shoe firms, as they were then known—the phrase denotes a WASP stereotype, with conservative dominance—that were by that time anachronisms in an industry in which aggressive trading desks were becoming *de rigueur*. Moreover, the merger left the resulting firm somewhat Balkanized, with different partners carving out separate fiefdoms. When two former Blythe partners left to found their own private investment firm, Gilford Securities, they asked Chanos to come along as a financial analyst, and as he was far more interested in researching the stock market than in doing-the-deal books to which he had been assigned, he said yes.

Shorting Defined: A Brief Primer for Those Who Have Never Traveled to the Dark Side

"Short" a stock and you are betting that the price declines; this is the opposite of being "long" a stock, when your wager is that the stock price will move higher. But the mechanics of these two types of transactions are very different.

Buying a stock is easy; just be willing to pay a price per share that someone is willing to accept in return for selling you his/her shares.

Shorting is much more complex. First, your broker must locate a "borrow"*— that is, find a shareholder willing to lend his/her shares to you with the promise that you will return them at some indeterminate point in the future. In return, the lending shareholder receives what is tantamount to an interest payment. This common transaction, "selling short," means that you are selling shares that you do not actually own (but have borrowed) with the promise of ultimately buying those shares in the open market at a point in the future to "cover" your short. Your hope, of course, is that you will be returning the shares at a lower price, capturing the difference as a gain on the short sale. The lending shareholder, of course, hopes you are making a bad bet. Here is an illustration:

You have been watching a company, which we will call MovieStream. The stock price is $100 per share, and the

---

*Most shareholders do not even know they are lending their shares out. The way it often works is this: A large index fund has many billons under management. In return for a fee, they provide the stock loan inventory to your brokerage firm, or your brokerage firm has its own large inventory, which could be its customers' stocks that are held in Street name. They get a call for a "locate" of shares to borrow, and then they lend the shares to the short seller.

price-to-earnings ratio—in shorthand, the P/E—is nosebleed high at a 50 multiple. In the course of your continuing research on the company, you come across a trade publication that mentions that a few companies are poised to launch competing services. Justifiably, you determine that Movie-Stream stock will come under pressure, so you decide to initiate a short position. Your research proves correct; the share price declines to $50 per share. At this point, you cover the short by purchasing the shares in the market, returning them to the shareholder. You have a nice gain of $50 per share. What was an original liability of $100 per share is now a profit of $50. And of course, the person who has loaned you the shares has suffered a loss in the same amount.

Now let's look at the other possibility. The trade publication was wrong; there is no competing service coming onto the market, and it is unlikely there will ever be. The stock ultimately trades to $150 per share, translating into a $50 loss on your short position and a corresponding increase in the liability you owe on the shares you borrowed. When a short goes against you, the position gets bigger; when a long goes against you, the position size shrinks. If your total portfolio were valued at $1,000 and you were short $100 in MovieStream stock, it would be 10 percent of your portfolio; if it trades at $150 and the short goes against you, it's 15 percent of your portfolio.

And then there are the "crowded" shorts, where a large percentage of the share float has been borrowed by short sellers. Occasionally, these trades do work out but often cause a lot of pain to the short seller. Short interest is regarded as significant if it reaches more than 10 percent of the float, but it is not uncommon to see stocks with a 20 to 25 percent short interest. Crowded shorts can be extremely volatile

(Continued)

because any hint of good news in the underlying fundamentals may create significant upward pressure in the stock price as weak short sellers scramble to cover, often in spite of the overall negative case still being intact. Broad market rallies can also pressure shorts just as broad market sell-offs cut a wide swath in depressing stock prices. In fact, a strategy employed by some traders is to scan the market for stocks with large short positions and buy shares, hoping to "squeeze" short sellers by forcing them to cover as they seek to limit their losses from a rising share price. Keep in mind that the potential loss for a short seller is infinite since the stock price can always move higher while the potential loss for a long holder is limited to loss of capital should the stock trade to zero.

The Baldwin-United Short

The first company Chanos researched was an oddball creation called Baldwin-United, a former piano company that had, in Chanos's words, "morphed into a high-flying financial services company." Its biggest product was the single premium deferred annuity,[2] sold through Wall Street brokerage firms, and it was this product above all that made Baldwin-United the absolute darling of Wall Street equity analysts. It constituted a new paradigm, was a fresh and different way of doing business, and always beat earnings.

Chanos was not as sanguine as other analysts, especially when he got a tip from a disgruntled insurance analyst who had questioned Baldwin-United's management and had then been effectively muzzled through concern about job security.

Chanos pored over the company's required disclosure statements and found that they failed what he calls his Rule of Three—namely, "If you read a financial disclosure three times and cannot understand it, it is intentional." Following the insurance analyst's tip, he also plowed through a batch of letters from the relevant state insurance commissioner—the company was headquartered in Arkansas—to Baldwin-United management. In the letters, which had been requested under the Freedom of Information Act and were available to the public, the commissioner had asked a number of questions about the firm's solvency.

In fact, all the research Chanos did was in readily available documentation—a central lesson he imparts early to students at the Yale School of Management, where he lectures on finance. It meant that everything damning about Baldwin-United, as he says, "was hiding in plain sight."

And a lot was damning. A professional analyst, fluent in balance sheets, accounting records, and all legally required financial documents, Chanos simply could not figure out how the company made its money. The records made it clear that it was not earning "anywhere near" enough to pay out the annuities it was selling. Worse, the state insurance agencies were allowing Baldwin-United to "front-load all its future profits"; this meant the company could show instant profits on the books, while in fact it was bleeding cash to pay the brokers for selling the annuities.

Jim Chanos was a kid in some people's eyes—a babe in the woods, just a couple of years out of college. So maybe he just didn't know that negative reports were not written. It simply wasn't done, especially on a company such as Baldwin-United that was adored by Wall Street. It was everybody's favorite growth stock, had been featured on the cover of *Forbes* magazine, and represented an exciting innovation in financial services. Nevertheless, when Chanos took his negative report on Baldwin-United to his seniors at Gilford, they stood by him and followed his recommendation to short Baldwin-United's stock. They did so for the simple reason that Jim Chanos had the evidence. Beyond the required 10Q and 10K[3] reports, he had the memos that company management had written, which detailed how to front-load the profits; he had the letters from the

Arkansas insurance commissioner expressing concerns about solvency; he had looked at the numbers and had documented his case with references, citations, footnotes—that is, with the facts.

Chanos issued his report on August 17, 1982, a date less memorable for Chanos's publication than for the fact that it was the exact moment the stock market experienced the "intergalactic bull market," as Chanos calls it, that kicked off the stock market boom of the roaring 80s. "Timing," says Chanos, "was never my forte, but I'm still proud of that report."

It is fair to say that Gilford clients were not thrilled with the timing either, nor with the short—at least at first. But as the weeks rolled on, the facts on Baldwin-United received more attention. By October, the *Wall Street Journal* had picked up the story and had begun asking some of the same questions Chanos was asking. Chanos now began to feel the lash of the counterattack from analysts and other interested parties refuting his case. Unable to assail the facts, they fired on the messenger. He's a novice, many said of Chanos. He has no insurance experience. He has never met with management. He doesn't get it.

This was the first, but by no means the last, time Chanos would hear himself pilloried.[4] At least he wasn't totally alone; he continued to have the backing of Gilford's leadership, and he had the facts. When *Forbes* set out to do a major piece on Baldwin-United, its editors challenged Chanos to "walk them through" his report. He did so, and while the magazine found no "smoking gun," its article took Chanos's case seriously.

The light bulb really went on for Chanos when a key Wall Street analyst directly refuted one of Chanos's claims in a way that made him realize the analyst had never looked under the company's hood at all. The realization prompted Chanos to recommend that Gilford management double down on the short—on the theory that if no one was willing to look at the truth, it was going to hurt even more when it surfaced—and management concurred. Baldwin-United's stock soon plummeted, and the short paid off handsomely.

Retribution for Jim Chanos followed on Christmas Eve. Chanos was back home with his family when he got the phone call telling him that the state of Arkansas had stepped in and seized Baldwin-United and all its assets. It was a moment of some satisfaction.

Future decisions in life are most often dictated by prior experience—both success and failure. Win the first time at the blackjack table and you keep coming back in an attempt to replicate that experience. For Chanos, it was the positive experience he had with his first short sale, which, unlike blackjack, was steeped in skillful analysis and shaped his path. He has never looked back. The Baldwin-United short made his reputation, and the pattern he set in identifying the important facts hiding behind the distractions became his signature.

Short Seller Supreme

Lured by Deutsche Bank, Chanos finally moved to New York. He began looking into the Drexel Burnham companies run by junk-bond king Michael Milken and recommended shorting them. Milken is a genius who created an entirely new way of financing companies. Built upon a mountain of debt, when company fundamentals and the economy are strong, leveraged entities can provide great returns, but when either deteriorates, look out below. Chanos was among the first to point out the dangers of this financing mechanism and focused on some of the less creditworthy companies. Charges flew that Chanos and other short sellers indulged in slippery tactics, and Deutsche Bank senior management got nervous. Big firms, with their varied business lines and multiple constituencies—in other words, company politics—often consider other factors than pure performance. This misguided attack resulted in Jim losing his job. But he had been right about Milken's Drexel Burnham companies, and the short was eventually profitable.

He founded Kynikos Associates in 1985 as a short selling firm, suffered some serious losses, and registered some major wins. Kynikos shorted commercial real estate in 1986 through 1992, shorted real estate again in the bubble leading up to the subprime crisis, shorted Boston Chicken, Sunbeam, Conseco, Tyco International, and of course in 2000 came up with what seemed at the time one of the most stupefying shorts ever: Enron.

The parallels between Enron and Baldwin-United, says Chanos, were "eerie." Once again, Enron was a company on the cutting edge, having found a new way of doing business, beloved by Wall Street, making money hand over fist, and becoming the name on everyone's lips. And as with Baldwin-United, "everything was hiding in plain sight," Chanos says. "You just had to look." And look he did, at a time when Enron was the darling of Wall Street, generating massive fees and lulling analysts and shareholders into visions of eternal gains on their investment in the company. Enron's Chairman, Kenneth Lay, was one of the most respected executives in corporate America; it was almost heresy to question him.

Chanos questioned, and Chanos probed. It was a big, big win, and it brought him an even more stunning level of fame as America's preeminent short seller.

Doggedly—and Successfully—Cynical

As Jim Chanos welcomed me into the office of Kynikos—a place where books spill off the shelves—he is as sunny and charming a host as can be imagined. Easygoing, articulate to the point of eloquence, a superb storyteller, Chanos exudes goodwill, and his cheerfulness and elfin smile evidence a most contented man, not necessarily the personality one might expect from a legendary short seller.

Short sellers tend not to be the best-liked people in the room. Their presence brings the shadow of catastrophe to a stock, making them the most unwanted of guests—especially at a party that everybody else is enjoying to the hilt. They may suffer the sad solitariness of being the lone voice in the wilderness, and it is a voice an awful lot of people simply do not want to hear. Those people tend to blame the messenger. John Mack, then the CEO of Morgan Stanley, famously did it during the financial crisis of 2008. Dick Fuld, former head of Lehman Brothers, agreed.[5] But what everyone loses sight of is that short sellers don't make the news; that is to say, they are not the ones who create the negative fundamentals. Rather, they exist to identify and profit from the holes in an investment thesis that others overlook, either intentionally or from lack of effort.

Short sellers are cynics, questioning all they see. The word cynic derives from the Greek, *Kynikos*, inspiring Chanos to choose the name Kynikos Associates for his company. Roughly translated it means dog-like but its etymology is much more expansive and on point. The followers of the ancient philosophers Antisthenes and Diogenes met in a gymnasium in a place called the Kynosarges. On the outskirts of Athens, the Kynosarges had been designated for use by those who lacked pure Athenian blood, so from the start, the Cynics were seen as outsiders. It was in the gymnasium that Antisthenes, labeled the Cynic philosopher, preached to these followers. Their philosophy spurned wealth, and its adherents often made a point of rejecting conventional manners and living on the streets, adding to the perception of Cynics as dog-like—idiosyncratic, contrary, tenacious. Not coincidentally, these are the qualities, absent the austere lifestyle and aversion to wealth, a short seller must possess to profit in a world dominated by markets that are most often optimistic.

"A short is a hedge that should produce positive alpha," says Chanos. "It's an insurance policy that pays premiums." Kynikos Associates' dedicated short funds have done just that over the quarter-century plus since Jim Chanos founded his business. The fund manages $7 billion in two portfolios, one U.S.-based, the other global. Each portfolio is comprised of just 50 positions.

Risk management, so essential to a short seller, is managed through position limits. Says Chanos: "The two ways to handle risk on the short side are stop losses or position limits. Stop losses don't work for us, both for trading and emotional reasons. Once you exit a position, it's hard to re-enter it." Instead, no position in the portfolio is ever at more than 5 percent. "If it hits five," says Chanos, an automatic trigger "cuts it back to four and a half." Sizing, he says, is as important as research "once a stock is in the portfolio." Even the firm's biggest disaster—its short of AOL in 1996 to 1998—"was never more than a 1 percent position."

To be sure, the name of the game is always to look for the negative. To that end, says Chanos, "all our work is forensic." Chanos and his small but exceptionally experienced staff, which includes some former investigative reporters, do not talk to company management. "CEOs don't know or shouldn't tell you their predictions for the future," says Chanos. "Corporate management is no better and arguably worse" at outlook prognosis than anyone else.[6] Instead, "We start with the spin," he says, and what follows is an exercise in intellectual honesty.

"In the last 30 years," Jim Chanos asserted, "every major financial fraud has been uncovered by an internal whistleblower, a journalist, and/or a short seller—or some combination thereof. Not by the SEC. Not by law enforcement. Not by internal auditors or counsel." It is why he believes short sellers are essential to keeping the world of finance honest; they are, in Chanos's phrase, "a market-incentivized group that can root out fraud." That emotions run high around shorting and short sellers is surprising to Chanos only in the sense that the practice itself is so quintessentially rational—and that is all to the good. "Short sellers arguably are the ultimate capitalists," says Chanos. "Without us pointing out failures, the capital markets won't function as well."

The China Short

There is no lack of irony in Kynikos's canine association and the firm's legendary short of China since, as is widely known, dog is still a menu item in some parts of the People's Republic. Yet this is a case where the diner may end up being swallowed; that, at any rate, is the big bet Jim Chanos embarked upon in the fall of 2009.

The path to Chanos's China short was indirect. The firm had been exploring the abnormal returns of some producers of iron ore and other commodities. The returns were "so far above historical norms," Chanos says, that he decided to investigate further. It turned out that "80 percent of the marginal demand came from China, despite its being only 10 percent of the world economy."

Chanos directed his staff to uncover the reasons for this, and they found the answer in the number of square meters of class A office space—that is, high-design, top-quality, high-profile office space—under construction or in development. The number was 2.8 billion square meters. "You must have transposed the decimal point," Chanos said, interrupting the analyst making the presentation. "That's what I thought at first too," the analyst replied. The number was correct.

Chanos did some quick mental figuring: 2.8 billion square meters is roughly 30 billion square feet, he quickly calculated, and 30 billion square feet, given the population of China, means a five-foot by five-foot office cubicle for every man, woman, and child in China—a totally absurd proposition. "That's when the enormity of this unprecedented building wave struck me," says Chanos. "This was building stuff for the sake of building it."

True to form, he investigated further. What numbers might the Kynikos analysts have missed? Which numbers weren't real? The research was fast but thorough and uncovered two standard "myths" about China, as Chanos calls them, that needed "to be addressed and refuted."

One myth is the migration argument—that is, the idea that with 20 to 30 million rural Chinese peasants moving to the cities, housing is desperately needed. The need for such housing is indeed desperate, although Chanos suspects that the number of temporary workers moving from villages to cities is actually higher than the 20 to 30 million figure given, but the point is that what is being built is not affordable housing; rather, it is high-rise, high-priced condos that can be afforded by only the top 2 to 3 percent of the population. The construction boom, Chanos concluded, was "all speculation."

Chanos is somewhat sympathetic to the speculators. The real estate market in China, he recalls, only got started in the late 1990s; it isn't very old, and it has only gone up. The market has "no experience with empty construction, no sense that it depreciates," says Chanos; moreover, "there is no secondary market." For reasons of both cultural legacy and future profitability, everyone wants to own a new condo, and there are plenty of them to buy. But, asks Chanos, "to whom will they sell the ones they've bought?"

Meanwhile, the speculative boom "is doing nothing to alleviate the housing problem for the low-wage laborers" still pouring into the cities.

Bottom line: "Supply is now consistently outstripping demand."

The second myth, says Chanos, "is that nobody is leveraged." Again, partly due to cultural legacy and partly to credit controls—at least theoretically—by the central government, there is the assumption that everyone in China pays cash. The truth, Chanos found, is that "credit growth is exploding in China." Since municipalities may not issue debt, local officials partner with a developer and set up a local government financing vehicle that can borrow the money for marquee development projects. Small businesses, to which big banks may not extend loans, find credit in an active, if hidden, black-market environment for down payments and small loans. Chanos found that even large corporations had begun to use corporate cash to speculate in the real estate boom, setting up property subsidiaries to do so.

Kynikos's research estimated that credit as a percentage of GDP in China has averaged 20 to 25 percent per year as far back as 2003; some estimates put total private credit in China at 200 percent of GDP. In fact, no one knows how many loans are outstanding. The government has made repeated efforts to tighten the credit markets, making it more difficult for banks to lend and for people and corporations to borrow, but both the lender and the borrower have done end runs around those government efforts. The shadow banking system in China is estimated to be near $1.5 trillion, an astoundingly large amount of credit to be sloshing around. But the bulls on China don't seem to care, as Chanos asserts, since any debt that goes bad is backed by the central government; at least that is the escape hatch the China-is-the-future boosters count on. Still, backing that kind of outstanding debt could be an awfully big pill for the nine-member Politburo in Beijing to swallow, especially since the local governments have every incentive to keep the speculation going.

Even given the haphazard nature of some of the data on China, the assumption that there is missing data, and the large grain of salt with which short sellers typically receive handed-down assumptions, any way Chanos sliced the facts and no matter how skeptically—even cynically—he looked at them, "You could see the magnitude and the direction" of the construction boom: "It was big and going up." Kynikos eventually estimated the size of the property market at more than 60 percent, when including related activities, of China's total GDP—absolutely unprecedented, Chanos believed. "Something unique in world history was happening," he concluded. "A world-class bubble was being inflated right before our eyes just two years after our own bubble had burst."

He saw it as "one giant land boom," in Chanos's phrase. "Land underpins all of it. It's the basis of the municipal finance; it's the collateral for all the loans; it's the value-added on all the real estate. And if it goes, a big part of the Chinese economy goes." On that basis, starting at year's end 2009 and in the first months of 2010, Kynikos began shorting the Chinese property market. It has been, he says, "a very good short."

Chanos takes pains to insist that his short is contained—limited only to the Chinese property bubble, although he contends that he believes the Chinese growth model overall "has problems and needs to be navigated." His bet, however, is against the boom. Benchmarked inversely against the indices, the short focuses on developers, banks, commodity suppliers, even railway companies tied to the bubble and trading in Hong Kong or elsewhere.[7] But Kynikos is, Chanos says, "economically long the market." Specifically, the firm is long Macau casinos. In other words, says Chanos, whether out of cynicism or sheer irony, he is "long corruption, short property."

As we go to publication, China's economy is indeed showing signs of slowing. Various economic indicators are showing signs of contracting and hitting recessionary levels. Property surveys indicate that transactions are slowing and prices declining in most major cities. Demand in China's most significant export market, Europe, is also declining. Through all this bad news the China bulls voice the mantra that the central government will not allow the country to suffer a hard landing. The United States, far more experienced than China in the ways of capitalism, could not prevent a recession, yet the U.S. market expectation is that a still communist country, much newer to capitalism, will be better at managing their slowdown.

Putting your money on the eternals of human nature rather than on the ephemera of an infatuation—especially one based on murky "facts"—may or may not be the quintessential short seller move. It is certainly quintessential Jim Chanos, especially when accompanied by the fruits of dogged research. And while he may be almost alone in saying what he is saying and investing against what everyone else is certain is the wave of the future, would you bet against him? Table 4.1 may help you answer that question.

Table 4.1 Beware: The Global Value Trap

Classic Short Selling Themes	Value Stocks: Definitive Traits
• Booms that go bust	• Predictable, consistent cash flow
• Consumer fads	• Defensive and/or defensible business
• Technological obsolescence	• Not dependent on superior
• Structurally flawed accounting	management
• Selling $1.00 for $2.00	• Low/reasonable valuation
• Value traps	• Margin of safety using many metrics
	• Reliable, transparent financial
	statements

Table 4.1 *(Continued)*

Value Traps: Some Common Characteristics	*Current Value Traps*
• Cyclical and/or overly dependent on one product	• Liquidating Trusts
• Hindsight drives expectations	• Digital Distribution Destruction
• Marquee management and/or famous investor(s)	• Miseducation
• Appears cheap with management's metric	• Nationalistic Commodity
• Accounting issues	• China Bubble Fuel

Vale (NYSE: VALE): China or Bust?
- Cyclical peak creates impression of value
  Forward P/E 5.1x*, operating cash flow margin over 45%
  $160/ton iron ore price more than 5 × 30-year historical average
- Capital expenditure inflation is soaring—2011 budget of $24B; up 85% over 2010
- Questionable capital allocation—VALE Navy
  12 Chinamax 400k dead weight ton very large ore carriers ("VLOCs")
  "It's not our policy to make money in freight."—*Jose Carlos Martins,
    Vale Executive Officer of Marketing, Sales and Strategy*
- Enormous exposure to uncertain Chinese demand growth
  China accounted for 43% of Vale's iron ore sales in 2010, up from 29% in 2008
  Reliance on continued fixed asset investment growth in China
- Brazilian Government influence on strategic decision making
  Key driver of economy—iron ore exports accounted for 17% of total exports in 2010
  Recent resignation of CEO Agnelli amid rumored tensions with newly elected government

---

*Source: Based on Bloomberg estimates.
Source: Excerpted from a speech given by James Chanos to the Value Investing Conference, October 17, 2011.
Source: www.valuewalk.com/2011/10/
jim-chanos-full-presentation-investing-congress-2011/#ixzz1fmCLNFq6.

The Takeaway

By definition, a hedge fund makes simultaneous bets on investments that its managers expect to increase in value and on positions they expect will decrease in value, hoping to profit from both. By being hedged, they hope to be in a position to make money regardless of market direction. But ask any hedge fund manager what is the most difficult aspect of investing and he or she will admit that it is "finding shorts that work."

There is a codependency between the words "shorts" and "work." It is not too difficult to find a company whose fundamentals are declining, but the trick is finding one whose stock price has not already been discounted for a turn in fortune. Small companies are usually more fertile ground for shorts since they are generally less well followed, but a fund the size of Kynikos requires big positions or multiple positions relying on the same theme to make an impact on its overall performance. And then of course there is the ability to be patient and to absorb losses on the way to being right so that you can ultimately book the gain. Very few hedge funds, and certainly very few individuals, have the fortitude to stick with a short position; it is certainly easier to take the path of least resistance and follow the herd. Imagine always going to a movie and rooting for the hero to lose. The world is full of optimists, thankfully, and markets tend to rise more often than decline, making Chanos's consistent performance all the more remarkable.

All of which helps explain why short sellers are always in the minority. And like a number of minorities, they are maligned and shunned by the legion of long shareholders and their army of supporters—including Wall Street analysts and company managements and, recently, even government regulators who have occasionally banned the practice of selling short. Being a short seller is lonely and often gut-wrenching. Being good at it requires having the constitution of a competitive eater. But unlike Joey Chestnut, perennial winner of the Nathan's July Fourth hot dog eating contest, a short seller's holding period can extend to weeks, months, or years before claiming the win. And instead of an antacid, the medication is additional research and correct position sizing.

The most important aspect of Jim Chanos's success is, in fact, research—an extensive process that provides him with the fortitude to stay with a short position even when the price action goes against him. With accounting shorts or frauds such as Enron, there is rarely a slow atrophying of the stock price as investors continue to buy into what they believe is a solid fundamental story. All the while, the fraud is working to do what it is designed to do: make the investment extremely attractive. Enron's Ken Lay spun a web that captivated investment bankers, analysts, and investors, driving the stock price higher and higher. Investors—and of course Enron employees as well—were entranced by a fairy tale that Aesop would have been proud to write.

Much like an individual investor, dedicated short sellers don't have access to a company's management team to vet their thesis. Companies don't want to speak with someone who only wins if they lose. So Chanos relies on his own grassroots research efforts, including a top-to-bottom review of all financial filings of both the company he is targeting as well as of others in the same business. If, for example, every company in a particular sector has an operating margin of 15 percent, how is it that one company, with no special products, has an operating margin of 20 percent? To those bullish on the stock, this is great news; no questions need be asked. But to Chanos, this is a yellow flag. Maybe the outsized margin is justified, maybe not, but it is in any case worth a look. He

(Continued)

and his team of analysts will then research the thesis from the bottom up and the top down. As the last step in the process, Chanos convenes a meeting with his analysts and elicits their input, exhorting them to poke holes in his thesis, while he tries to find the weak links in theirs. Having already checked out the firm's ability to borrow the shares, they start building the position. It is critical that they do it stealthily lest other funds compete with them for the "borrow." Once Kynikos has a full position, they sit and wait for the story to unfold, for others to see what they see, and find out what they already know, on occasion sharing their information with others.

Sometimes, as with WorldCom and Enron, Chanos has targeted a fraud; more often, it is a story unraveling from the top down, as with China. Or it could be that a company's business model is flawed and there is a large discrepancy between deteriorating fundamentals and the high valuation accorded to the stock price by the market. To the extent the market closes this gap, Chanos makes his money. But it does not always work out, or it doesn't happen quickly enough and, as mentioned before, he can suffer a great deal of pain in the interim. So how does Chanos or any other short seller stay the course when the overwhelming majority is going the other way?

Shorting stocks is a tough business and not for the faint of heart. It requires independence, an appetite for risk, and deep pockets. Make a mistake in buying a stock and the downside is defined; the lowest it can go is zero. But short a stock and the loss is theoretically unlimited since the stock can continue to trade higher. The practical application of this is that when a short goes against you, it becomes a bigger part of your portfolio; when a long position doesn't work, it becomes a smaller part of your holdings.

There are two basic types of shorts: fundamental and valuation. In the case of Enron and China's banks and property developers, Chanos found significant flaws in the investment thesis of each. With both, he could help make other investors aware of these issues and perhaps decrease the time he would have to wait to get "paid" on his investment. After all, he was extremely confident in his work and could point to the catalysts for his negative thesis to come into play. But shorting stocks solely on the basis that their valuation is too high, that they are "too expensive," is a dicey strategy. Valuation shorts are a different matter since there is no identifiable catalyst to drive the stock lower.

For example, let's say you come across a stock that is trading at an egregiously high and unsustainable level based on virtually any valuation metric. Let's suppose, for example, that this particular equity is trading at a price/earnings multiple of 75 at a time, when the average P/E of all the stocks represented in the S&P 500 market index is 15. Sure, the company is growing slightly faster and has a great balance sheet, but you determine that such a large valuation discrepancy is unwarranted. You continue digging and cannot really find any flaws in the story, but that doesn't matter since you believe the company will eventually have a misstep and then everyone will realize that the stock price is just too expensive. Besides, how much more expensive can it get? You decide to short the stock and then you wait. And wait. And wait. The stock drifts higher, and now the pain of loss is palpable despite the stock being more overvalued than when you first put the position on. But, as previously noted more than once, here is the issue: The market can be irrational for a longer time than you can stay solvent. Valuation shorts, without any identifiable catalyst

(Continued)

within a defined period of time, can often result in significant losses.

Back in 1999, during the Internet stock bubble, a smart hedge fund manager I knew shorted Amazon. At the time, the company was barely making a profit, and the P/E was almost incalculable. My fund manager friend could not find anything wrong with the company per se. Yes, it was a relatively new concept, and analysts' projections for growth were mind-blowing. But this fund manager was accustomed to owning stocks that traded at a P/E of 10 to 20 times, not 100 to 200. So he shorted the stock at $100 a share, then shorted some more at $125 a share, and more at $150. Finally, after losing millions of dollars, he covered his short and learned the valuable lesson that it is very difficult to make money on valuation shorts.

The conclusion reached by many is that shorting stocks is the bastion of hedge fund professionals. In fact, for the most part, I agree. But if you still want to engage in the practice of short selling because you are absolutely convinced that a particular stock is overpriced, there are two strategies you may want to consider. The first is buying puts where the potential loss is defined by the cost of the options. The second strategy is to wait for the stock to "break." Tops and bottoms in stocks and markets are virtually impossible to predict with any certainty or consistency. But once a company's fundamentals turn, once that unidentified catalyst actually becomes visible, the momentum is broken, and the price often begins its precipitous decline. Once the emperor is shown to have no clothes, his most loyal subjects—that is, the shareholders—desert the investment in droves, driving the price lower. At this point, the biggest risk, albeit uncommon in application, is that another company acquires the entity you have shorted.

The final takeaway: Shorting may not be the riskiest form of investing, but it can be the costliest. It is a science, not an art, and very few investors are successful at it. Most professional money managers don't short stocks because of the inherent risks. But if you are a completely independent, non-consensus thinker who has the wherewithal to perform in-depth research and maintain strong risk controls, have at it.

Notes

1. Author's comment: I believe that China will be a growth opportunity for many years to come and holds unbridled economic promise. However, managing the transition to a more capitalistic society will be bumpy and expectations of the transition will periodically exceed reality. I do not believe anyone doubts the growth story, Chanos included; the skepticism relates to what an investor should pay for it at a point in time.
2. A single premium deferred annuity is a contract between an individual and an insurance company in which the individual provides funds that are invested and later used as the basis for lifelong distributions to the annuity holder.
3. The Securities and Exchange Commission requires public traded companies to file a quarterly (10-Q) and annual (10-K) financial reports.
4. Short sellers are often targets but never more so than during the financial crisis of 2008–2009 when Congress took up the cry against them. Short selling of financial stocks was banned for a period of time.
5. John Mack and Dick Fuld blamed short sellers for bringing on their issues of solvency, never owning up to the fact that it was likely a lack of proper risk management that nearly bankrupted their firms. What neither Mack nor Fuld pointed out was the significant amount of revenue their companies earned from facilitating the activities of short selling firms.
6. As Chuck Royce will mention in Chapter 6, he feels no need to speak with management prior to initiating a position, preferring not to be biased before doing his analysis.
7. Within days of completing this interview, China's major sovereign wealth fund bought shares in four Chinese banks in an effort to shore up their capitalization, the result of a deteriorating financial position as loan losses increased.

Chapter 5

Digging Deep, Coming Up Big

Lee Ainslie

I t is fitting that the big win Lee Ainslie is willing to talk about is a highly successful investment that his firm, Maverick Capital, made in a technology company. Technology is how Ainslie became interested in stocks in the first place.

He was 14.

An investment club had started up at his school, and the club members wanted to track a number of early computer stocks. It was the era of the Commodore PET, of Radio Shack's TRS-80—known lovingly as the "Trash 80"—and of the legendary Apple II. Do-it-yourselfers, a large number of whom were schoolboys, were tireless in the creative uses to which they put BASIC, the Beginner's All-Purpose Symbolic Instruction Code that was the first accessible language of computer programming. Young Lee Ainslie asked the teacher guiding the investment club if he could write a BASIC program that would track the stocks the club had interest in. The teacher said yes, and Ainslie wrote the program. He has been tracking stocks ever since.

He has also been investing in them with stunning success—first at the fabled Tiger Management Corporation, headed by his mentor, Julian Robertson, and then at the hedge fund he created in 1993, Maverick Capital, consistently recognized as one of the top funds in the world. Nevertheless, it was through being what Lee Ainslie describes as "a computer nerd," that he discovered and embarked upon his life's work.

The work is stock picking—pure and, if not simple, certainly classic. It is the classic purity of the process he applies and the sheer depth of the research he does that distinguish Ainslie and Maverick. Neither pure process nor depth of research is out of character for this soft-spoken southern gentleman with the analytic bent and competitive nature.

Nurturing a Tiger Cub

The school with the investment club and the early foray into computer programming was Virginia Episcopal School. Lee Ainslie went on to graduate from Episcopal High School, also in Virginia, a venerable institution known for its association with such historic figures as Walt Whitman, for its honor code, its religious focus, and for the rigor of the education it offers. He was not just a student there; he was part of the family. His father, Lee S. Ainslie Jr., for whom the school's current arts center is named, became the headmaster shortly before Lee's senior year. So it is probably safe to say that the things the school stands for—its serious educational purpose, high ethical standards, and meticulous discipline—quite naturally became part of young Lee's extended DNA.

He took it all with him to the University of Virginia, where he concentrated on courses that fit his analytical bent, graduating with a BS in Systems Engineering. After college, he went to work for the head of information technology at KPMG Peat Marwick, exercising his penchant for technology. Perhaps being the son of a headmaster and understanding the value of education had something to do with it, or perhaps it was just an unquenched thirst for more knowledge, a trait that would be the hallmark of his investing style. But whatever the motivation, Ainslie left his consulting career and enrolled at the University of North Carolina's Kenan-Flagler Business School in Chapel Hill.

Returning to the South was a fortuitous move for Ainslie, for it was there at UNC that he encountered Julian Robertson, at the time a member of the Board of Trustees of the university and, as it turned out, another Episcopal High School alumnus. Robertson attended UNC as an undergraduate and had been managing a portion of the university's endowment for some time. Rightfully credited as one of the pioneers of the hedge fund industry, Robertson founded Tiger Management in 1980, overseeing investor assets of $8 million. By the late 1990s, Tiger's assets under management would swell to $22 billion.[1] Robertson must have taken note of the young guy with the familiar name, for when Ainslie had graduated and was "looking around for opportunities," Robertson called and invited him to New York for an interview.

Still a young firm at that time, Tiger was seen by many on the Street as an unconventional—even aggressive—upstart, not the natural choice of an MBA grad looking for a career in finance. Ainslie, not to put too fine a point on it, could probably have had his pick of established financial institutions to join. "Go with a Goldman Sachs-type firm!" he was advised by more than one well-meaning confidant. "There is no better experience for your resume." Ainslie listened, letting all the well-intentioned advice seep into his still-open mind. He flew to New York on a Wednesday, essentially interned at the Tiger offices on Thursday and Friday, and was offered a position the next week. His decision process was less tortuous than that of the people whose counsel he sought; in fact, for Ainslie, it was as simple as a college athlete deciding to go pro. "There wasn't anything else I'd rather do. Somebody was going to pay me to do what I loved to do. It was no contest." Thus, Lee Ainslie began his career as one of the early investment professionals of Tiger Management Corporation. He started hedge fund life as a generalist, but would eventually specialize in technology, his old standby.

Apprentice to Journeyman to Master

For Ainslie, the time at Tiger was the equivalent of an apprenticeship. At first, he worked closely with consumer analyst Stephen Mandel, another Robertson protégé and the founder of hedge fund giant, Lone Pine Capital. By the end of his first year, however, Robertson asked Ainslie to focus on the technology sector. It was 1990, and not too many people were interested in tech companies or tech stocks. But Robertson apparently understood the investment potential of the technology industry, and he certainly sensed that Ainslie understood the role of technology itself.

It was exciting to take on this role at such a young age—Ainslie was 26—and at such an early point in what would undoubtedly be an enduring career. "The downside," he says, "was having to develop expertise in a wide range of quickly changing companies, but the upside was that I had very few preconceived notions." He was baptized into what he calls "the Tiger mentality." It consisted of "finding the best business with the best management team and thinking in terms of years, not quarters. So you would end up picking a Cisco or a Microsoft, where most firms were more focused on which companies were going to beat the next quarter, which is a very tough way to add value consistently." And, Ainslie might have added, probably not nearly as profitable or effective. Hedge funds are often mistakenly painted with a broad brush, as hair trigger traders seeking to make quick profits. But Tiger, Maverick—in fact, most hedge funds—are the antithesis of fast acting, preferring to take a very long term view. It is a cause and effect relationship with investments; the recognition that they have to be early to a story since that is when the opportunity is the greatest and the understanding that it will take patience for the fundamentals to unfold, the combination of which should result in strong performance.

Every stock pick had to go through Julian Robertson, and typically months of work preceded a presentation to him. "Julian was a quick study," Ainslie recalls, "and halfway through, he could say, 'Okay, buy it.' But if he didn't agree, he would let you know that too." Persuading Robertson, however, was, as it should have been, a tough assignment that took all the intellectual rigor, analysis, breadth of scope, and presentation skills that Ainslie or anyone making a pitch could muster. There probably could not have been a better course of training in the business of selecting investments and building a portfolio than the work Lee Ainslie carried out at Tiger— the research, the questioning, the probing, the study, the re-examining, the putting it all together. It was a lifetime of learning compressed into three short, exhilarating years. (While at Salomon Brothers, I was responsible for the day-to-day relationship with Tiger and it was akin to dealing with a team of all-stars.) When, in 1993, Texas entrepreneur Sam Wyly approached Ainslie and asked him to run a money management fund he was seeding with $38 million of Wyly family money, Ainslie felt he had to listen. It was a chance to do prematurely what he knew he wanted to do at some point in his career—run his own firm. That fall Maverick Capital was launched. While Ainslie managed the stock portfolio, Wyly managed debt positions for the first 17 months. By early 1995, the firm had sold off all its non-equity positions, leaving Ainslie solely in charge of the portfolio. In 1997, he acquired a controlling interest in the firm.

Mapping Maverick

Ainslie is aware that his pursuit of success at Maverick can become all-consuming. He admits to growing antsy as Sunday afternoon rolls around—"I want Japan to open so the game will be back on." When you are running an operation that by definition ignores regional boundaries and time zones in seeking out the best investment opportunities, the clock offers little respite. With financial markets more widely dispersed than ever before across a truly global economy, there is always a market open somewhere, always a data point emerging that Ainslie and his colleagues don't dare miss. While Maverick is not a trading firm, the drive to stay on top of information that affects the portfolio is in the partners' blood. Garnering information before others is a critical edge in Maverick's pursuit of generating high returns and preserving capital. All of this takes a significant amount of time. In order to guarantee that he is left with worthwhile time to spend with his family, he limits his civic and philanthropic activities almost exclusively to chairing the Board of Directors of the Robin Hood Foundation, a weighty responsibility that he takes very seriously as the foundation redefines the way donors and grantmakers target poverty in New York City. To further ensure quality time with his family, he built Maverick to perform using a teamwork model so that "it is not dependent on any one individual." In turn, when he is at work, he is there 100 percent. His competitive self would have it no other way.

While others contribute to Maverick's success, it is still the firm Lee S. Ainslie III created and built according to his own specifications. Right from the get-go, he knew just what kind of process and culture he wanted it to have.

First, he kept it simple. It was to be a classic equities-only fund, in which short positions were to be true investments, not just hedging mechanisms, balanced with long positions within each industry sector and in the context of a net long fund. Deep and exhaustive research was to provide the competitive edge, and a peer-group team-based culture was to make it all work. Perhaps building the culture was the most daunting task of running the business, not just because of the nature of hedge funds but of money management firms overall. Often, the biggest gains in a portfolio are generated by going against consensus and finding the idea that everyone else hates or chooses to ignore. This requires a certain independence, a willingness to stand up and profess love for a stock while a vocal majority casts aspersions on the investment case you are making. As the name suggests, Maverick reveres independence. It seeks to build, within a team framework, an opportunity for the oft-ignored loner voice to be heard and for independent thought to be considered. This approach has worked extremely well, averaging an annual return of 17 percent from the time Ainslie stepped away from Wyly up to the financial crisis of 2008. The years 2003 and 2005 were marked by underperformance and Ainslie took note of the reasons, learning some key lessons. In 2003, low interest rates had undermined the firm's short positions—a lesson about the power of external macro forces. In 2005, the trouble wasn't macro trends but a weakening of the team culture, according to Ainslie's analysis. Sector teams had become isolated into separate silos and had grown unwilling to assume sufficient risk. It's a flaw Ainslie has worked hard to correct. Then 2011 hit, another down year for Maverick, but one that proved extremely difficult for a number of otherwise top performing funds.

Maverick's investment team started out consisting of a single professional—namely, Lee S. Ainslie III. Today, it consists of 55 investment professionals. See Figure 5.1.

The investment team is driven by six industry teams—healthcare, technology, consumer, cyclical, retail, and financial—which have global responsibility. Each sector head of these six teams is an expert in that industry—the current sector heads average nearly 20 years of experience in "their" industry—and represent an unparalleled resource of knowledge about the industry and of relationships with industry movers and shakers. In addition to these industry sector teams, Maverick has quantitative research, credit, small cap, privates, and

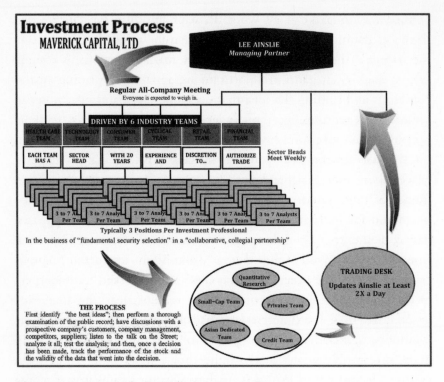

Figure 5.1   Maverick Capital's Investment Process

Asian dedicated teams. All are in the business of "fundamental security selection." As Ainslie neatly puts it, "Every business decision is based on how it impacts our ability to deliver returns to our investors." Figure 5.1 tracks Maverick's investment process.

Driving this simple model is what Ainslie describes as a "collaborative, collegial partnership." He further expounds on the culture, "I'm a partner of the firm, and there are many important partners." All are rewarded by "how we do as a firm, so there is an incentive to help one another."

The structure reinforces this principle. While each sector head has discretion to authorize a trade, every investment team—

comprising typically from three to seven analysts—meets weekly; all the sector heads meet regularly; and there is a regular all-company meeting as well. Ideas are aired, virtually from the moment they're conceived, and everyone is encouraged—indeed, expected—to weigh in. The idea is to plant and sustain a holistic view, in which varied seeds of intelligence can be germinated and nurture one another.

Ainslie is in touch with the sector heads throughout the day, sits in on most meetings, and gets an update twice a day or more from the trading desk, which he regards as the firm's "eyes and ears on the market." Industry sector professionals glued to a computer screen is, he says, "the last thing I want to see." After all, Maverick is not in the business of responding to market movements but rather to bottom-up fundamental data points. Whether the market is up or down one, two, or three percent is immaterial to the Maverick investment thesis on its individual holdings; it is only noise. But investment firms cannot operate in a vacuum, and the trading desk is the firm's finger on the pulse of the market—and on world events that may affect the markets. Leaving the news updates to the trading desk both frees the investment professionals to concentrate on the long term and gives Ainslie a direct and up-to-the-nanosecond line on what's happening in the wider world. At day's end, the Maverick team sifts through company, industry, and macro updates and evaluates each position in terms of whether or not it is as good a use of Maverick's capital today as it was yesterday. They try to identify what he describes as "the best ideas" about where Maverick should be investing in an effort to decide how much capital should go where. As Ainslie learned from Julian Robertson, the test of a decision is buy versus sell; there is no hold option. The choice is made every day, either by default or by volition. The meaning is clear: Every day the equities markets are open for trading your portfolio is alive, and by holding onto a position you are very much making the statement that you would buy it again that day.

Feeding this daily decision making is a body of exhaustive research, considered by the market—and by Ainslie—as a prime competitive advantage of Maverick Capital. As he famously told two McKinsey interviewers in 2006, "Our goal is to know more about every one of the companies in which we invest than any non-insider does."[2] It's a good bet Maverick meets that goal.

The research is gathered via a method that typically takes a few months before an initial purchase and could then require many months to build a full position. The professional staff performs a thorough examination of the public record, has discussions with a prospective portfolio company's customers, discussions with its management, discussions with competitors, discussions with suppliers, and listens to the talk on the Street, analyzing it all, testing the analysis, and then, once a decision has been made, tracking the performance not just of the stock but of the validity and effective use of the data that went into the decision. Apart from everything else, tracking exactly how each decision worked out in terms of cold, hard performance is a way to continually refresh and improve the Maverick process and its culture. The process may be said to start with the fact that the number of investment positions per investment professional is typically about three—a distinctive depth of diligence right there, enabling a very high concentration of research. The point of this is that in order to take a position, it has to be concluded that the new holding is the best use of the firm's capital, and in concert with the requirement to know more than anyone else about what the firm owns, the number of holdings per capita could be said to be limited by Maverick's process.

"We're a team of peers," Ainslie asserts. "There is no king of the hill." It makes for a distinctive environment, and as Ainslie concedes, "There are many talented people who do not enjoy such a team-oriented environment." Those who do, however, rarely want to leave; at the senior level, turnover has been negligible. To build depth of bench, however, the firm recruits a pool of candidates from among "second-year" performers at the top investment banks, consulting shops, and corporations. A winnowing process narrows the number of applicants in the pool, and these candidates are then interviewed and tested. After reviewing the results of rounds of interviewing and testing, a select number of finalists are invited to take part in a final day of interviewing, which typically starts at 7:00 in the morning. The applicant is given a computer and presented with a case study to evaluate and about which to offer a conclusion. "We see what they can do with it," Ainslie states. The applicant goes on to a series of interviews with the senior partners, each conversation probing the candidate on "a different component of success at Maverick," components that have been identified as key to the work—logic, rationality, emotional consistency, the ability to cope with stress, among others. In return for this fairly grueling process, new hires get a two-year commitment plus training.

Not surprisingly, Maverick has kept data on which hires were recommended by which senior partners, so that "Years later," Ainslie says, "we can see who was right." It is," Ainslie repeats, a matter of "improving the process."

The Cognizant Big Win: Challenging Conventional Wisdom with Research

It's safe to say that in the year 2000, when then–CEO of General Electric, Jack Welch, spoke, people paid attention. Some of the tech analysts who would wind up at Maverick listened attentively when Welch proclaimed his 70-70-70 rule for GE: 70 percent of technology processes to be outsourced; 70 percent of that 70 to go overseas; and 70 percent of the overseas 70 to go to India. By 2002, the Maverick tech team, under the leadership of Andrew Warford, started looking at one of the original Indian information technology outsourcees, Cognizant.

The selling points were obvious: Claims that outsourcing could save one third of the cost of business processes were common, and

in the late 1990s and early 2000s, with the economy stumbling, businesses were desperate to reduce costs. Conventional wisdom, however,
held that the desperation was overblown, had run its course, and
would soon be on the wane as the economy in general improved.
The Maverick technology team thought otherwise. They posited the
thesis that the cost-cutting outsourcing experiment had seen such
strong results in terms of savings, with work that was equal in quality
to, if not better than, what could be produced in-house, that customers would actually do more outsourcing, not less. In fact, Warford
and the team believed that the initial, tentative, somewhat tepid flight
to outsourcing was actually the start of a long-term trend, and that
Cognizant represented a technology-enabled business that could be
instantly exported and that would grow accordingly.

Then they set out to test the thesis.

Step one was to talk to customers. How is that done? It's a bit
like detective work: You make a call, get a lead, follow it, get another
lead, and keep on digging. In the case of Cognizant, Maverick's
researchers talked to customers that represented more than half of
their revenues, interviewing chief information officers all over the
world. What they learned was stunning: Virtually every customer
they talked to said they planned to expand their business with
Cognizant in the succeeding year. "That increment alone," Ainslie
reports, "was the growth Wall Street expected for the whole
company"—without Cognizant adding a single new customer. Says
Ainslie: "We had never seen anything that powerful."

Step two of testing the thesis was to talk to competitors—mainly
Infosys and Wipro—and managers at both painted a picture of stable
pricing and heavy demand for their services, in contrast to the
common Wall Street concern of margin pressures on the business. In
any event, the research found that Cognizant's operating margin in
the low 20s was significantly lower than its competition. This created
a margin of safety relative to competitors that established greater
earnings stability and allowed room for incremental investments
versus the competition.

Step three was to kick the tires of management. In trips to India, as well as in meetings with Cognizant management in their U.S. offices, the tech team reviewed the financials and discussed the company's strategies for maximizing shareholder value and for dealing with potential pressures on margin.

Finally, in step four, the Warford led team talked with suppliers—specifically, with outplacement firms and universities—for a view of what employees entering that job market needed and could look forward to.

The research confirmed their thesis that Cognizant was positioned for growth in an industry about to take off and, in January 2003, Maverick built a substantial position in Cognizant stock, buying at a price of slightly less than $5 per share.[3]

Positioning the shares in the portfolio never marks the end of Maverick's analytical process. In fact, says Ainslie, "The due diligence was ongoing for the full four-and-a-half years that we owned the stock." Such ongoing research, essential at any time, is particularly important in the case of a new business, which Cognizant was, in a new industry, which outsourcing was, in order to keep on top of threats and opportunities. And even though the research can become more efficient over time, it is, says Ainslie, "like mowing the biggest lawn in the world"—just as you finish up, the grass has already grown too long again back at the beginning, and you have to start all over.

Besides, as noted earlier, there is always a data point popping up somewhere. Maintaining acuity on a non-U.S. stock presents a particular challenge; it is not just the company one has to stay on top of, but also local government laws, changing regulations, and the region's operating environment. Some of these changes may be meaningful, so it is critical to know about them when they first bubble up, before the investment case is impaired. Without a local presence and boots on the ground, Maverick had to work that much harder to stay informed, and given the size of the fund's position, staying informed was critical.

Principally because Cognizant was a company based in India, the stock price was volatile, but with the long-term view that Maverick's depth of research and stability of assets made possible, that was understood and accepted. Peaks and valleys were within the realm of the position's risk/reward profile.

The time came, however, when the position was no longer as good a use of Maverick's capital as it had been the day before. There were two basic reasons for this. First, Cognizant's growth had begun to slow somewhat, a natural and expected occurrence, and second, other investors had caught up to Maverick's once non-consensus view on the future of outsourcing. At the intersection of those realities, maintaining the position no longer represented the best investment relative to other opportunities. In the investment business, as elsewhere, good things usually come to an end, so in July 2007, Maverick sold Cognizant, having realized an eightfold return worth "several hundred million dollars" in profit—a big win by any measure.

There is a postscript: As of this writing in 2011, Cognizant, priced at some 15 times what Maverick first paid for it, is back on the Maverick radar screen and back in its portfolio.

Analysis: Ainslie's Big Win

Maverick's investment in Cognizant generated such a high return because there were fewer funds able and willing to buy the stock with the confidence such an investment required. This paucity of buyers created an inefficiency in the Cognizant stock price versus the value that could be realized if the investment case played out as Maverick's analysis had forecast it would. At the foundation of the firm's success on this stock, as with so many of its successes, was Maverick's tried and true research process based upon the vast experience its analysts possess in emerging markets and their expertise in forensic analysis.

The Takeaway

At any level, retail or professional, investing successfully—whether in real estate, bonds or stocks—is a difficult business. But the pressures are even more intense when you are acting as a fiduciary, investing on someone else's behalf. Exhaustive efforts are required for even the most basic holdings. Now, imagine that an attractive investment opportunity sits half a world away. And it is the equity of a multinational company headquartered in a country that you have never visited nor know much about. The number of boxes to check on your due diligence list has just multiplied as if it were a school of guppies circling around a basket of chum that fell overboard. The country in which the company is based is threaded with business laws you never heard of, a tax structure you find opaque, labor traditions, commercial customs, and corporate cultures that make your head spin. Pretty complex, but wait—there's more.

Add in the fact that the company that has so piqued your interest is at the forefront of a relatively new industry, and its ability to gain traction with the world's top corporate entities is at the core of your investment case.

For the individual investor, attractive as that investment may sound, the challenge of pursuing it is likely to be beyond your capabilities and should therefore outweigh the attraction of the investment. Owning the equity of a company whose main office is based in a foreign country adds an entirely new level of effort if you're going to perform the required due diligence and ongoing maintenance of the holding. First, you have to be extremely well connected to be able to get grass roots information on a foreign company. Second, you need to have enough manpower to spend time in the environment

(Continued)

in which you are investing, tracking down all the necessary data points. Third, you will need to rely on local resources, including attorneys and accountants, who don't come cheap, to provide familiarization with the local laws and practices. The research effort does not stop once the position is put on; it is a living body of work that only dies when the stock is sold. While such effort is well within Maverick's capabilities, it is beyond the scope of most individual investors.

Although the sweet spot of Cognizant's client base was the Fortune 500 list of America's top companies, the focus of the research efforts was on the company itself, headquartered in India. A large amount of the due diligence could be accomplished from any location by reviewing financial documents the company is required to file with the Securities and Exchange Commission and to satisfy the listing requirement on the New York Stock Exchange,★ and over the phone—interviewing Cognizant's customers, for example—but there is no long-distance way to kick the tires, to ensure that a headquarters actually exists, to meet with multiple managers and discuss their strategy while observing their demeanor, their command of the numbers, and their confidence level. Numerous trips to India were required before the Maverick team felt comfortable with Cognizant management and their operational abilities.

For the vast preponderance of individual investors, just the cost of a trip abroad would be more significant than the capital put at risk in any one stock. And for a large number of professional investors, the time and all-in cost of a visit to Asia would make the investment unattractive. In fact, the

---

★This is discussed in greater detail in the accompanying sidebar. The filing requirements set forth by the SEC are, in part, dependent upon the exchange where the shares are traded; NASDAQ and NYSE have greater requirements than a Pink Sheets listing.

resources required for investing in companies domiciled in a different country are at the disposal of only a select few. Maverick is certainly one of that handful; the firm possesses the infrastructure, financial wherewithal, connections, and persistence needed to be successful.

But while there is generally no shortage of attractive investment opportunities in the United States, investors often seek to increase the potential field of possibilities by expanding beyond their own geographical borders. This is for good reason: The hallmark of an emerging market investment is faster growth, which can lead to higher returns; the downside is that because these companies are usually less mature, a higher risk profile is almost always present. And the strange bedfellow in this equation is greater volatility, a roller-coaster ride few individuals are willing to sign on for as the story plays out.

Retail investors who seek emerging market exposure, therefore, can buy mutual funds, and wealthy individuals also have the option of investing in hedge funds. But any direct investment you enter into by cutting corners on due diligence is riskier—and is not recommended. Granted, plenty of successful investments have been committed to with less, but such a strategy can rely more upon luck than skill. As Maverick's investment in Cognizant demonstrates, it really only works the other way around—that is, by relying on skill rather than luck although a little of the latter never hurts.

And that's the takeaway from this chapter. Direct investment in emerging markets should be based on experience, comprehensive due diligence done on the spot as well as through other research, and expert forensic analysis. In short, leave it to the likes of Maverick.

They are not alone in possessing this expertise, of course, and since the time of the initial foray into India, global

(Continued)

investing has become more popular, stimulating the creation of numerous funds that specialize in emerging markets. Individual investors should check on the credentials of the funds they invest in when seeking emerging markets exposure. The fund's client service team is usually willing to walk a potential shareholder through the process. However, if they are not forthcoming and do not make a potential investor feel comfortable with their methods, then they should be avoided.

Emerging Markets—Not for the Faint of Effort

Imagine you are nearing the roller coaster at Six Flags, not an average loop-de-loop roller coaster but rather one of those super-duper ones that causes you to strain your neck as you follow the path of the tracks, the one that you look up at and say "no way" as your kid drags you by the arm and says, "c'mon, there's nothing to be scared about. I'm just a little kid and I'm not afraid." Reluctantly, you shuffle forward to confront your fears. Beads of sweat form on your brow as you say a silent prayer while waiting on the platform, standing on your tiptoes to look down at those who just boarded the ride in front of you as they fall from sight into that first, steep drop. You flinch, convinced that that there is no way those cars will stay on the track. It is finally your turn and you weigh the risk of a possible derailment with the reward of making a memory with your child, that brave, but clueless, little person standing by your side. The ride begins and you are haunted by second guessing as you embark upon that first drop to what you are convinced is certain death, your knuckles turning white as they clench the bar braced against your chest, the only barrier to unplanned flight. Elation follows at having conquered your fears; then another climb, straight up this time, up a wall of worry, followed by an even steeper, more sudden drop as your stomach mimics the movements in nauseating exactness.

Welcome to the emerging markets. Strap in—it can be a wild ride. The volatility in emerging markets and, consequently, in emerging market equities is a fact of life. Perhaps volatility is no longer unique to emerging markets since big intraday swings in indices have become endemic to all equity markets, even those in developed regions such as the United States, Japan, and parts of Europe. However, a degree of comfort can be taken in the regulatory oversight of companies domiciled in developed nations. But even the oversight that comes with being headquartered in the United States is not sufficient to quell the impact of local influences when a company has virtually all of its operations in a less developed and less regulated market. It is not only the prospects for hyper growth, often followed by a hyper fall, that causes the volatility in emerging markets; there is a contagion that often controls sentiment, regardless of black and white results. The capital markets in these countries are viewed as opaque, often accompanied by distrust, so at the first sign of market weakness, traders cut and run. Fortunately, as governments realize that they require the flow of capital into their countries to help drive industry, and thus growth, they begin to put in more controls. However, some are still a long way from providing investors with enough comfort to draw them in.

While risk is always present in an environment that is perhaps more wild west than developed western nation, opportunity for return is often born in a prima facie opaque environment. The fact that Cognizant is based in India, a

(Continued)

country not known as a role model for regulatory oversight or corporate governance standards, provided an opportunity for those willing to look beyond conventional impressions and perform the appropriate due diligence—although few were adequately resourced to do so. However, once a firm like Maverick, known for its rigorous research process, appeared as a shareholder, others followed into the stock. (Following anyone into a position is a dangerous game; see Chapter 2: Follow the Money: The Ugly Reality of Whale Watching.) And once people understood that the entirety of Cognizant's business was with the Fortune 500, they assumed an additional degree of comfort, casting aside the doubt associated with India.* But what if it is the other way around? What if a company is headquartered in the good old U. S. of A. with the entirety of its operations in fast growing emerging markets? Isn't that the best of both worlds? One would think so but, unfortunately, the taint does not discriminate, yielding a very wide brush of skepticism and uncertainty. Therein lies the case of NII Holdings (OTC: NIHD). I have owned NII Holdings off and on for a number of years and I have the twitch to prove it.

NII Holdings† is a cellular services company headquartered in Reston, Virginia that operates exclusively in Latin American markets including Brazil, Peru, Mexico, Chile, and Argentina. Originally part of Nextel Communications, it became a standalone entity in 1997 and its customer base is almost 100 percent business. Churn, that is, customer turn-

---

*I would actually argue that Cognizant is not a pure emerging markets growth story, given their customer base; at some point the calculation on valuation is a comparison to American companies with some discount applied given their foreign domicile.

†For illustration purposes only: This is not a suggestion or recommendation to buy shares in NII Holdings.

over, is extremely light, better than most U.S. companies. Typical of a cellular company as it builds out or upgrades its network, NII Holdings has a significant, although manageable, amount of debt on its balance sheet, but it also has a great deal of cash. With 14,000 employees in the United States and Latin America and nearly 10 million subscribers, it is comfortably on the membership roster of the Fortune 500. Additionally, NII Holdings is 197th in the Barron's list of the top 500 U.S. domiciled companies as ranked by revenues. Revenues are just shy of $7 billion and the market capitalization is approximately $4 billion. The company has grown revenues and EBITDA* in the mid-20-percent range for a number of years. Not exactly an unknown entity, the company is followed by more than 20 brokerage firms.

Get the picture? NII Holdings is one heck of a company. Strong, stable management, inexpensive valuation at just over three times EBITDA, and U.S. based management operating in some of the fastest growing emerging markets in the world, including Brazil. So why then has the stock, as of this writing, been cut almost in half over the last year? The growth rate far exceeds that of most other companies, particularly those with a market capitalization of $4 billion or more. Sprint (NYSE:S), by comparison, has a horrendous balance sheet with significantly more debt relative to cash, has much stronger competitors in AT&T and Verizon in a much more mature market, has a negligible growth rate, and

---

*EBITDA = Earnings Before Interest Taxes Depreciation and Amortization. EBITDA is a proxy for operating cash flow. EBIT, Earnings Before Interest and Taxes, is another valuation metric and proxy for cash flow preferred by certain investors. Both are discussed in Chapter 6 on Chuck Royce.

(*Continued*)

loses money, yet the market accords it a much higher valuation.

What gives? Sprint is also based in the United States and essentially all of its operations are domestic. There are no foreign tax laws or business regulations to worry about, no little known and unpronounceable competitors, and all of the important analysts that follow Sprint are based in the United States and are easily accessible to fund managers. While NII Holdings has a large research following, most of those analysts follow Latin American equities and do not speak to the same investors who look at Sprint. And there's more.

More than occasionally, it seemed to me that NII Holdings was the stepchild to both the Latin American and U.S. markets. On days when the U.S. markets rallied, NII Holdings would sometimes trade lower because of an occurrence or rumor in Brazil or Mexico, their two largest markets. I always feared that the analysts and traders based in Latin America had an edge in information flow. In fact they did, even if it was knowledge as basic as what could be culled from reading the daily Spanish language newspapers.

For all of the above, NII Holdings was my roller coaster, making my stomach churn with aggravation and the constant sensation of being the last to know. Fact is, I often was. I would periodically check in with the company to see how business was progressing and chat with some of the analysts who followed the stock, but frequently I found that their information lagged the local markets. NII Holdings did not seem to be a priority for them. Even representatives of the company told me on occasion about their frustration with the inconsistent coverage. They want more U.S. analysts to follow the stock, but they recognize that they are more consumed with stocks like AT&T and Verizon and Sprint, a function of what their clients want to hear about. The U.S. based analysts felt at a competitive disadvantage to analysts that were fluent in Spanish and based in the regions where NII Holdings did business. And it was not because management in Reston, Virginia, is native Spanish speaking*; it was because the competitors to NII Holdings were, and so were the regulators who presided over wireless licenses. They operated in a different time zone, and the die was cast for the trading day as news broke while the New York analysts slept.

That is yet another issue in emerging markets that should not be overlooked—news stories break and stocks trade in reaction while most of us sleep. Making money while lying prone on 400-count cotton sheets is not always a legal activity, but it is for emerging markets investors. Conversely, it can also be a money losing experience. Granted, that same feeling of helplessness often occurs right here with stocks on the New York Stock Exchange, since most companies wait until after the close of trading to release news that will cause big moves in the price of their shares, but I digress. Nonetheless, it is a circumstance about which every emerging markets investor should be aware, since it does add to the stock's volatility and possibly ratchets up the risk quotient as well.

Here's the point: I have been around a long time, my experience greater than many, and I find investing in emerging market companies to be distracting, often times frustrating, but at other times very rewarding. I am prepared to do the extensive, ongoing due diligence required, to hunt down the rumors, to seek out what is behind—if anything is behind—the wide day-to-day swings in the price of the stock that will imbue me with the confidence to stay with my

---

*In place in each country where NII Holdings does business is an indigenous management structure, including a President of Operations. This is particularly important in certain countries where the business and legislative communities are close knit.

(Continued)

holdings in the face of the volatility. But you have to ask yourself—are you?

Assume that NII Holdings is a one-off example. It's not, but let's also stipulate that it is neither a U.S. company nor a true emerging markets holding. Let's instead focus on an emerging markets domiciled company with a stock that also trades in the United States. Cognizant, of course, is an example of this, but what about a company that is not as big or does not have such a stellar roster of customers? Some investors believe that buying the equity of a foreign company that has listed its shares on the New York Stock Exchange, or on NASDAQ, puts it on equal footing with a company head-quartered in the States. This is absolutely false. Granted, the exchanges and the Securities and Exchange Commission (SEC) require a significant amount of financial information before allowing the listing of a foreign company's shares on the major exchanges, but this alone is not to be mistaken for the Good Housekeeping Seal of Approval. The transparency require-ments for an American based company such as NII Holdings are much greater. More important, however, there has been a loosening of the filing requirements for foreign companies that trade on the Pink Sheets★ in the OTC market.† While

---

★Companies trade on the Pink Sheets because they are either too small to meet the minimum requirements for listing on a national exchange or they do not want to provide the financial disclosure required by the SEC. So named because the listings were originally published on pink sheets of paper, these securities are more prone to manipulation and are often "penny" stocks—small market caps and often priced below a dollar per share.

†Exchange Act Rule 12g3-2(b). This rule provides an exemption to certain filing requirements for foreign private issuers in order to "remove needless barriers" to U.S. capital markets. This amendment to the original rule provided for the electronic transmission of certain filings, making the information more accessible to the average investor.

these basic filing requirements do weed out some of the more obvious potential frauds, the SEC and exchanges do not perform due diligence on any company for their suitability as investments, nor do they have the time or responsibility to audit their filings. In fact, there has been a recent spate of companies headquartered in China trading on U.S. exchanges that have caused significant losses for both retail investors and institutional money managers. Specifically, these China based companies acquire a publicly traded U.S. company and merge their business into what is largely a corporate shell, thereby doing an end run around lengthy, rigorous, and complex filing requirements. This process obviates the need for an Initial Public Offering, not a good thing for potential shareholders since it also impinges upon what is usually the best opportunity for an investor to become familiar with the business through significant disclosure.

Consider yourself informed about the trials and tribulations of emerging markets investing and turn now to the reason why a portfolio should have exposure to this segment of the global markets and how to gain entry. The reason to have exposure is simple: Faster growth will lead to high return. By definition, emerging markets are in the process of undergoing a positive change to their capital and business environment that will provide for stronger economic growth than that in more developed nations. These burgeoning economies have a smaller base upon which to grow, except for China, which already has a very large economy, but one where the per capita productivity has significant upside. This period of relatively stronger growth will be reflected in higher market returns. How to be involved? It seems to me that the most efficient and risk-appropriate way to participate in these markets is through an investment in an emerging markets

(Continued)

fund. The portfolio managers of these funds have an expertise in these markets and the resources to allocate to the due diligence process. Very few individuals have the financial wherewithal to invest in a hedge fund like Maverick, but there are many emerging markets mutual funds with low minimums available to the everyday investor. The advantage of these funds is that their holdings are diversified among many regions. Of course, if you are predisposed to a particular geography, there is no shortage of funds that will concentrate your risk while still being diversified among different businesses and industries.

But if you still prefer to be your own stock jockey and like tugging on the reins yourself, there are ways to play emerging markets with less volatility through companies such as Yum! Brands (NYSE:YUM). Yum! is a casual dining restaurant that has established growing operations in China and India. Or put an oil company in your portfolio that benefits from global commodity exposure and increasing energy usage as economic growth accelerates. Of course, the true risk is ultimately dependent upon the individual stock.

Notes

1. Putting this in perspective, a hedge fund at the time was considered extremely successful if it had $1 billion under management. Now, of course, the extreme success of those early days is a *paltry* sum that barely throws off a living wage for most hedge fund managers. In fact, there are a few who take home a billion in wages each year.
2. Richard Dobbs and Timothy Koller, "Inside a Hedge Fund: An Interview with the Managing Partner of Maverick Capital," *McKinsey on Finance*, no. 19 (Spring 2006): 6–11.
3. Maverick does not concentrate its portfolio. It keeps positions to less than 5 percent of the firm's equity.

Chapter 6

small caps, BIG GAINS

Chuck Royce

Remember the kid who from age six knows exactly what he wants to do when he grows up—and then grows up and does it? No adolescent angst about a future identity, no senior year *what's next* bull sessions in college, no doubts or detours. The things he wants to do in life, as well as the person he intends to be, are completely obvious to him from virtually the moment he becomes conscious of the wider world, and this certainty lends a kind of self-assured serenity that most of us simply do not have.

Chuck Royce has that serenity, not only, it seems clear, because of his extraordinary success and unquestioned wealth, but because he went about doing exactly what he has always wanted to do, never for a moment wanting to do anything else, and he is still doing it daily and joyfully, with appetite and with vigor. What Royce does, of course, is pick stocks. He has been doing it since the 1950s, and he does it very, very well. What is particularly distinctive about him is that he does it so very well in the segment of the stock market inhabited exclusively by small capitalization stocks—*small caps*, as they are commonly called for the sake of brevity. The standard cliché about small caps is that they are too risky and too vulnerable to fraudulent practices, that they lack quality, and that they comprise a growth-focused niche that does not really outperform companies with higher market capitalizations. Royce gives the lie to every bit of that cliché. Today, as President and Co-Chief Investment Officer of Royce & Associates, Chuck Royce has achieved an enviable legacy of performance that has consistently shattered the usual assumptions about small caps, an accomplishment that confers *legendary* status, particularly given the size of his business. The Royce Funds include more than 20 mutual funds with total assets under management of $40 billion, all of it allocated to investments in small-cap value stocks.

In person, Charles M. Royce's appearance belies his accomplishments in a business known to chew up and spit out those with much more intimidating personas. Shoes off in the office, where he likes to do research, bow tie loosened, he is low-key and welcoming; there is no hint here of the snarl of a world-beater, little outward evidence that this is a guy who threw down the gauntlet against proffered investment wisdom and won. Nor did Royce set out on a path of conquest. His prominent presence in the investment world has a more romantic beginning than that.

It happened when he was a high school student growing up in Maryland. He was in the school library one day, browsing through the reference section, when he happened upon the big green loose-leaf binder containing the weekly *Value Line* investment surveys, a stock analysis newsletter to which just about every library and brokerage firm subscribed. He "thumbed through" the binder, in his words, and that was it. "I fell in love with the idea of stocks." Stocks, then and even now, as hedge fund managers vie for attention with rock stars, are an unusual recipient of the amorous yearnings of a teenaged boy, but love often has its roots in serendipity.

Royce himself can find no rhyme or reason why this thunderbolt of passion should have struck him. His father was a civil servant in nearby Washington and his mother a schoolteacher; by no stretch of the imagination did either of them play the market, nor was investing a common topic of conversation around the Royce dinner table. Royce vaguely remembers wondering why his grandfather never worked, and he recalls escaping from Thanksgiving dinner at his grandparents' house one year, rummaging around where he should not have been rummaging, and coming upon a box of funny-looking papers he would later recognize as stock certificates. But investing in stocks was not something that was in the air or in his background unless one subscribes to Mendel's theory[1] on recessive genes to explain why young Royce's interest in stocks seems to have been inherited from his grandfather. However, given that there is not yet a DNA test for inherited stock picking ability, the thunderbolt in the library, like every experience of falling in love, remains as inexplicable as it is profound.

It also prompted action. Young Chuck turned "the idea of stocks" into reality by actually buying one—Syntex, one of *Value Line*'s hot glamour picks, the first manufacturer of the birth control pills that were to transform behavior and revolutionize the culture. It was the first and very possibly the last time Royce put his money on a high flier.

The wherewithal to buy the stock was earned in the usual way—a paper route, summer construction work, odd jobs. "I always felt comfortable financially," says Royce, so you can cross out covetousness or an inferiority complex, in addition to the urge to conquer, as first causes for his interest in stocks. Rather, "Something in my nature loved thinking about the process," Royce says, "loved figuring the odds." Clearly, he understood at an early age what takes most investors years to come to grips with; stock selection is in fact a process, not a whim, not the result of chasing a fad or listening to a tout.

At Brown University, he first enrolled in engineering, the standard major for the go-getters in his class, then switched to economics—"it seemed easier." Royce added parimutuel betting on horses to his thinking about the process often visiting the two local tracks, both now defunct, "After a certain number of races, you could walk in for free," recalls Royce. He rallied his fraternity brothers, persuading them to pool their money, then calculated the odds and placed the bets. "It was a fine way to kill an afternoon," Royce says, "and I think we did pretty well." The betting also provided a very direct education in actuarial systems of risk assessment and management; the lessons—on whether and how well you beat the odds—having been learned in about the time it takes a Thoroughbred horse to run three-quarters of a mile. Not long at all.

Royce's economics studies certainly supplemented this hands-on learning, but what he loved most about Brown, where he now serves on the Board of Fellows, was the "atmosphere of intellectual discourse" that reigned there. Although today he relishes delving into the minutiae of research, back then, by his own admission, scholarliness was not his strong suit. In addition to the racetrack, there were the usual extracurricular distractions of the college experience. Also, like many young men in the late 1950s, Royce fulfilled his draft obligation through a ROTC program that he began in college—in his case, as a Marine reservist. With one summer spent training at the Quantico Marine Base in Virginia, a couple spent doing construction work, and one devoted to summer school to "true up" his course requirements, graduation soon loomed; it was time to move on and move out.

"Everybody went to business school in those days," Royce says, and since he wanted to be in New York City, he and a bunch of friends decided they would enroll in Columbia Business School, which was noted for its strong investment reputation and has over the years turned out a number of other legendary investors, Mario Gabelli and Lee Cooperman among them. There, at long last, he threw himself into the study of finance and investment. "It was absolutely what I wanted to do," he says; it answered the summons he had felt as a kid thumbing through *Value Line*, and he "just went through it, straight through," with no stops, no digressions, no summer internships, no uncertainty at all. "It makes a difference to go forward with an idea of what you want to do," says Royce, and as he grasped the MBA diploma at graduation, he must have had a sense that he was truly on his way.

On the Not-So-Fast Track

But when Royce looked for a job after B-School, he found roadblocks instead. It was the early 1960s, and the banks were in ascendance. That was where the best and the brightest wanted to be—specifically, in the highly coveted, hyper-elite credit training programs offered to the most sought-after recruits, and very specifically, in the training program offered by the Chase Manhattan Bank, then the most prominent financial institution in New York, if not the world.

Unfortunately, Royce was not accepted into Chase's training program, nor into any other bank's training program, but his admirable determination pushed him forward. As a large firm, Chase had many doors on which to knock for entry-level positions, such as their well-regarded Research Department. Once again, he was rebuffed. This second attempt would not be his last, since persistence is a common and necessary character trait for successful investing. This is particularly true when your playing field is small capitalization stocks, where information is not as readily available as it is for larger, more visible companies that are widely followed by the analysts at brokerage firms. Royce eventually landed a job at Chase as an analyst assigned to track lost dividends. This job, as one might imagine, was indeed forgettable, but at least he had his foot in the door at Chase and eventually qualified for a junior-level analyst position in the bowels of the Research division.

That was when the fun began. Chase, at that time, was "the kingpin of the investment world," in Royce's words, and he was in the middle of it, meeting people, exploring the many dimensions of investing, examining and assessing companies and their stock. A lowly junior analyst, Royce was like a kid in a candy shop, giving in to his brain's desire to wander, figuratively, here and there, exploring whatever research he thought worth probing—at least until his boss, a very senior utility analyst, suggested strongly that he should stick to researching the utility stocks to which he was assigned. Performing research on utility stocks, to be blunt, is often boring, since there is little that can go wrong or, conversely, go right enough to exceed expectations. And because they are supported by high dividend payouts that rarely change, the stocks typically trade in a very narrow price range. The sheer dependability of owning a utility removed the element of excitement from Royce's research role and did nothing to feed the intellectual curiosity that had originally attracted him to the investment process. Thanks to the stick-to-utilities admonition by his superior, Royce came to the conclusion that he was more a generalist than a utilities guy, and maybe he would be happier in a smaller firm where there would be other dimensions to his position.

This was the 1960s, more than 40 years before commission rates would decline to pennies a share and join with greater regulatory scrutiny to pressure profit margins and thin out the ranks of Wall Street firms. The brokerage business was still a growth industry back then, with new firms sprouting up everywhere. In fact, there were hundreds of small firms for Royce to explore for a role more to his liking. He landed at Blair & Co., Granberry Marache, a classic white-shoe brokerage house with a small number of branches and a fairly standard outlook on investing. Hired as an analyst by an investment research professional with considerable experience, Royce was given the opportunity to do "a little bit of everything" and he "really got to see how the brokerage business works." Royce recalls the invaluable lesson learned at this job: "This is a business where everybody rises or falls with the prosperity of the firm." Indeed, this knowledge would serve him especially well in his as yet unimagined future, where he would build a significant business enterprise of his own.

In 1968, Royce was lured away by an even smaller firm, Scheinman Hochstin & Trotta, where he was elevated to the position of Director of Research. This, he says now, "made no sense, as I was 29 years old." That may be too modest of Chuck Royce. After all, Wall Street has always been known as a meritocracy where age does not define an individual's value nor act as either a barrier or a guarantee to advancement. In fact, the firm supplemented his brief period as an analyst by also making him a broker. This meant that he now had customers to serve along with his research duties, something that today's regulatory and business practices would never allow. During what was the "Go-Go" decade of the 1960s, however, the regulators and regulations were fewer in number. Back then, the abuses were perhaps less obvious and the needed reform had yet to materialize; elected officials had yet to see the political and practical benefits of villainizing Wall Street. The first assignment for Royce was small caps, although back then, says Royce, "There was no such category. Small caps were just a more aggressive form of investing." It was also, as it remains today, a populous universe numbering in the thousands of companies, as well as being, in Royce's word, an "evergreen" universe, rife with new entrants in the form of both Initial Public Offerings—IPOs—and small companies spun off from bigger ones because they either did not fit with the larger corporate vision or were relegated to orphan status for one reason or another. Small caps, both then and now, can feel like the investment world version of a souk; they are as multiform, multifaceted, and multicolored as a bazaar in an exotic locale—and just as volatile. This was the universe in which Chuck Royce grew up as a researcher and stock-picker, and it is where he found a way of looking at the universe that allows him to understand which companies will perform with less volatility.

Royce thought mutual funds were "a fascinating business," so around the time he began to work at Scheinman, he and a childhood friend bought a mutual fund that had suddenly become "available." He reasoned that if other people were able to succeed at running a mutual fund, so could he and his buddy.

It was effectively a shell with no real assets and no real going-concern business. It consisted of a registration with the Securities and Exchange Commission, assets under management valued at less than half a million dollars, and a management contract. The fund had been created by twin Englishmen who had run it into the ground, forcing them to shut the doors. During their heyday, however, they had managed to purchase a country house in Pennsylvania, inspiring the name, Pennsylvania Mutual Fund. Royce and his friend decided to keep the moniker, since it "sounded very important" to them. Since Royce himself was directing research at Scheinman at this time, he was only a front man for the fund, taking the title of Chairman of the Board and leaving the day-to-day operations in the hands of his colleague.

The pages of the calendar turned quickly to the late 1960s, the era of the first no-load funds,[2] which helped attract more investment money into the industry. Assisted by this surge in capital, the Pennsylvania Mutual Fund did extremely well. In the course of two years, the value of its assets rose from virtually nothing to approximately $100 million—the equivalent of a billion dollars or more in twenty-first-century dollars. Then the landscape changed for the worse and, with recession taking its toll on the economy and on corporate earnings in the early 1970s, the overall market turned down, as did Pennsylvania Mutual Fund's performance. To make matters worse, disheartened by the market downturn, Royce's partner had withdrawn more and more from the day-to-day running of the company. At the same time, Scheinman merged with a now-defunct brokerage house, Weis, Voisin & Co.

Royce was conflicted; he wanted to hold onto his day job at Scheinman for the steady income, but that left him very little time to attend to his other business, which was suffering more and more every day from the effects of the bear market and his partner's withdrawal. So Royce was left to live with his own Catch-22. The assumption that "if others can succeed at this, so can we" was being sorely tested and found wanting, but Royce could do little because he felt compelled to stay with the job he believed offered him some security. Incredibly, Royce was rescued from this Hellerian dilemma in a twist that Joseph Heller himself would likely have admired, when a business disaster provided an unexpected escape.

The bear market claimed many victims as investors lost both money and confidence in the stock market. Weis, Voisin folded, as so many firms did in the early 1970s, and in 1972, with no more day job, Royce officially took over the Pennsylvania Mutual Fund.

It was, he concedes, a stressful period in his life. The market was doing badly, and so was the fund. Royce was married then, with small children, and "no money coming in." He began writing a column on investing for *Financial World*, which was at that time the granddaddy of U.S. business magazines; the work provided the only paycheck he could rely on.

And . . . it got worse. Now in sole charge of the Pennsylvania Fund, "I promptly lost whatever was left," says Royce—"40 percent in 1973 and another 40 percent in 1974," two years that were more or less a perfect storm of disaster for the stock market. Recession, inflation, Nixon—it was all there. So it was perhaps not surprising that at the Board of Directors meeting in September 1974, there was a strong feeling that perhaps it was time to wrap up the Pennsylvania Fund and liquidate the remaining assets. Royce summoned all of his persuasion skills and beseeched the other Directors to reconsider. He prevailed. The fund stayed in business. He had one more chance.

At the end of 1974, the stock market hit bottom. Then, pretty much beginning on New Year's Day of 1975, it began to take off. Royce's fund took off with it and beyond; in fact, it was up 125 percent more than the market. The outperformance was truly remarkable, a nice counter to the underperformance of the prior period. In theory and in truth, small cap stocks typically do worse than the overall market in bad times and better in good times—higher risk, higher reward, so the test of a portfolio manager in that discipline is often relative performance. Royce showed his mettle and then some, removing all possibility of debate as to whether it was happenstance or skill. With the usual ups and downs of the investing world, Royce's funds have been performing well ever since.

The lessons Royce has taken from that experience are crucial. The 1973 to 1974 time period was, as he bluntly expresses it, "just brutal" with the Standard & Poor's 500 stock index losing nearly half its value. His livelihood, and by extension, his dream of spending his life doing what he passionately loved, were endangered and almost lost. The message was clear: Chuck Royce understood that he "needed corrective therapy about how you mitigate risk." Of course he had always known in theory that "if you lose 50 percent, you have to make 100 percent"; that is, if you start with 100 dollars and lose half, you now have to double your remaining capital just to get even, a daunting mandate even in a strong investment environment. The events of 1973 to 1974 taught him that, as with so many of life's lessons where book learning is not a substitute for practical knowledge, "Unless you've experienced it, you cannot fully grasp it." He experienced it, and now he grasped it, and it became the core of what he calls the "vivid centerpiece of my investment style"—don't lose the money; risk control above all else!

Reaping Value

"The small-cap world is so large that you can do virtually anything you want in it," Chuck Royce asserts. "You can avoid clichés, can subsector the class any way you like to weed out things that don't fit and reduce volatility. The general perception is that small-caps are all growth all the time, with lots of volume. But the reality is much more varied, more nuanced."

Analyzing balance sheets, the core of the research process at Royce, requires precision. Paradoxically, there is no precise definition of "small cap." To Royce's point, there are many different small cap indices, including value and growth, each as a standalone index as well as value and growth combined into one.[3] There are also multiple indices against which a portfolio manager, such as Royce, can choose to be measured,[4] including the Standard & Poor's SmallCap 600 and the Standard & Poor's SmallCap 600 Growth and Value. Russell Investments, developers of the eponymous Russell family of indices and a competitor to S&P, uses broader metrics for inclusion in its multiple offerings of small cap indices. Equities in the Russell 2000 Small Cap index, for example, have a median market cap of $475 million, with the largest member of the index touching $3.7 billion, the smallest at just over $100 million.[5] The S&P 600, on the other hand, has members with market caps as low as $30 million.[6] Royce trolls for ideas in an even larger playing field, extending the definition of small cap to $5 billion, with the caveat that the funds may even invest in companies sporting a $15 billion valuation, although this would be unusual.

As we would expect of one of the pioneers of small cap investing, Royce makes some good points when expounding on his strategy. Arguably, small caps fall victim to a wide array of biases and investment ignorance; they are often lumped together in a group of stocks characterized as high-growth, with strong momentum, and are illiquid in terms of trading volume. But there is no definitive correlation between the market capitalization of a company and the trajectory of its earnings growth. Smaller companies can lumber along much the same as bigger entities. Conversely, one would be hard pressed to find a small cap company experiencing long term hyper growth similar to that of Apple Computer, which as of this writing is the largest company in the world as defined by market capitalization. And lumbering along, of course, does not evoke a vision of stock price momentum. Still, there is some truth to the view that seeking to enter or exit a position in smaller companies may require more patience, depending upon the number of shares or the total dollar amount of stock that trades on an average day. The dollar amount is more important because it is a true reflection of the capital at risk. Royce applied a whetstone to this large and varied world, honing it down to a selected reality of low volatility and high value. "Value" is not a word he particularly likes. In the investment world, he contends, it has become a cliché; overused, it has lost its meaning. In the wider world, it still means the worth or importance that a thing deservedly is held to possess, and in both the wider world and the world of small-cap investing, whether he likes the word or not, Chuck Royce knows value when he sees it.

The potential value of an investment can be favorably skewed by the eye of the beholder. When the Ocean House, the gilded-age hotel on the bluffs of Westerly, Rhode Island (the location of Royce's summer home) was sold to a developer who wanted to demolish the building and replace it with a row of McMansions, Royce stepped in. In tune with his investing discipline, the Ocean House is a relatively small hotel, the total size of which could possibly be overshadowed by the signage on a typical resort property. But Royce saw a communal, historical, and perhaps even a moral value in saving what could be preserved of a gracious past, and he also saw the social and concretely material value of transforming Ocean House into a new engine of economic activity. So that is what he used his wealth to do.

It is not too far-fetched to relate this instance of preserving and renewing value to Royce's core investment goal: "I am looking for sustainable, high returns on a company that is misunderstood in the marketplace, that I can buy cheaper than what it should sell for, and where I am buying into a compounding effect that will carry me a long way." A most critical component of Royce's thinking is that he is looking to buy *companies* not *stocks*; he analyzes each candidate for his portfolio as a business. To do that, Royce follows the discipline he put together out of the "brutality" of 1973 and 1974, and out of all the expertise and all the experience he has gathered in that "aggressive" small-cap universe.

Royce once described his discipline to an interviewer as a "carefully designed way of looking" at a potential investment, a way of looking that "can reduce volatility substantially" so he can "select portfolios that will perform better and with less volatility."[7] And, he might add, so that he may sleep better at night.

One element of the discipline Royce holds to is that "after Syntex, I now pretty much avoid high-flier glamour stocks." The reason? "The price you pay for stocks has a lot to do with how it's going to perform." Paying a premium for the sizzle, by definition, takes a hatchet to the value proposition, since the stock price reflects a possibly fleeting market infatuation with a particular stock. Glamour is an intangible, not found anywhere on the balance sheet and adding nothing to the intrinsic value of a company or its assets. And when the glamour fades, the stock price can start acting as irrationally to the downside as it did to the upside, when it was the darling of the often fickle markets.

With the avoidance of hype as a given, Royce regards the balance sheet as a particularly telling target of focus, with hard assets and cash being truly beautiful. It is a lesson he learned long ago, when he was head of research at Scheinman and he signed off on a favorable report on a company that promptly declared bankruptcy a month later. By his own admission, he simply "paid no attention to the balance sheet," which even a quick look showed to have accounting conclusions with holes big enough to drive a truck through. This was a lesson learned early in his career and with other people's money. Since that time, says Royce, "If I have only five minutes to look at a company, the balance sheet is what I check." But that is just five minutes of a much longer period of analysis, albeit a very important first step. Without a solid balance sheet, the hurdles to a stock making it into the portfolio become close to insurmountable.

He examines to what extent a company may be leveraged, since he looks for a company with sufficient return on assets to grow while minimizing debt. He looks at return on capital and at the interplay between income statement and balance sheet as tools of valuation of a company. When he thinks about what he wants to pay for a stock, he is an absolutist rather than a relativist. That is, he finds it less useful to see what others are paying for "equivalents" than to assess the company's standalone worth. The question he asks about the company is, "If I could own it, without any leverage, what kind of earnings could I take out of it?" The danger in being a relativist who compares two equivalent stocks, says Royce, is that "one stock is always cheaper, but what if both are overpriced?" As an absolute investor, he also expects to make money in absolute dollars, not simply "relative" to an index, although Royce does tend to beat the Russell—the aforementioned Russell 2000 stock market index that is the actual standard benchmark for small caps. Without the ability to make negative bets on stocks—that is, the ability to short—absolute performance is an unusual practical benchmark for a long-only manager, but it is the proper mindset since there is no solace in losing money for your investors.[8] But while no manager likes to lose money, asset allocators—the consultants who parcel money out to equity fund managers on behalf of pension plans and endowments—often judge a fund's success by how well it performs against their particular benchmark. So if the index they are measured against is down 35 percent on the year, as the S&P 500 was in 2008, and the fund only lost 25 percent of its capital, then the portfolio manager would no doubt see his fund size increase from the inflows chasing its relatively less poor performance. Essentially, outperforming mediocrity by the slimmest of margins is the benchmark for most funds, but not so in the case of Royce Funds. They strive for absolute performance, meaning they want to make money in all markets and take no comfort in losing less than others. It is an admirable goal, for sure, but one that has not always been achieved. I know many managers who take victory laps in being the best house in a pretty ugly neighborhood.

Because liquidity is sometimes an issue with small caps—these are not stocks that can typically be sold quickly or in volume—Royce must envision a higher return relative to the risk of not being able to sell out of a position when he wants to, which is the particularly onerous penalty an investor suffers when the investment case turns sour without much warning. Illiquid small cap stocks are the portfolio manager's version of the Roach Motel: You can check in but you can't check out. This is why it is critical to size the position appropriately and ensure that the stock price is supported by strong asset values.

It is on this "designed way of looking" at small caps that Royce has built both his formidable investing success and a distinctive and distinguished investment business. Naturally, there have been slow patches and down years. In the late 1990s, when everyone was climbing on the tech bandwagon, Royce did not; to do so would have violated his value discipline. Numerous investors strayed far from their discipline, lured away by the siren song of tech stocks that would double, often triple, even quadruple in price in very compressed periods of time. To those willing to forsake their discipline, the price action and return justified the strategy drift, a slippery slope indeed. "We avoided the tech ascendancy," he says, and although "we compounded nicely in the low teens, the market was compounding in the twenties. It looked bad relatively speaking, but we performed okay." Assets grew, but so did the number of redemptions, as mutual fund investors chased the performance of others. When the bubble burst, however, "we were proven right." Essentially, says Royce, "We changed nothing, but we no longer looked like a dunce." The market went into a steep decline in 2000 and 2001, "but we did very well during that period, as did anyone with a lower valuation approach." In other words, ignoring inflated price-to-earnings multiples and disregarding the risk of money-losing business models was no longer a winning strategy.

Today, The Royce Funds is a firm of about 100 people with offices in New York and Greenwich, Connecticut, and with some $40 billion in assets under management. The firm is "a big player in the small cap space," as Royce says, "but then, the small cap space is so big." It is a business built on making scale, collegiality, and an open atmosphere work. There are no "junior" people. "We don't do training here," says Royce. There is a particular environment—a particular culture—and the firm can move at a leisurely pace selecting people who might fit well in that environment. The interview-to-hire ratio is exceedingly high, the rigor and length of the process outlasting the time frame of many candidates. "You have to be comfortable working out of a cubicle in an open atmosphere," says Royce—there are no closed-door offices in the place—and it is a "very transparent process" in which "everybody is invited to every meeting" and nobody does his own thing. In fact, only two people have traditional offices, Royce and his long-time number two, Whitney George. But unlike conventional corporate hierarchies, there is no correlation between where an employee sits and compensation, since the portfolio managers can potentially earn millions of dollars a year because their bonuses are tied to their individual performance and that of the funds.

The firm also takes its time researching stocks and building a full position. While "taking a position can take an hour," says Royce, "taking a big position can take years." The equity may be so thinly traded that trying to put on a full position in a short period of time could drive up the price significantly. Then there is all that core research, and of course there is the chance to sit down and meet in depth with a company's management. Royce, however, is wary of the latter. As interested as he is in what he calls "the dialogue" of how a company got to where it is and about its strategy for the future, he is aware that you sometimes "can't help being snowed by 'wow' people." And CEOs got to be CEOs for a reason; they usually have powerful and persuasive personalities that can sway one away from objectivity. So Royce is content to take a meeting with management as "a piece of the puzzle" while believing that "results are results" and that they are available in the company filings required by the Securities and Exchange Commission. Once the stock has been purchased for the portfolio, of course, the firm is glad to be in regular communication with management.

That is the way it worked with Ritchie Bros. Auctioneers, the Canada-based industrial equipment auctioneer whose stock has been a big win for Royce Funds. It is an investment that epitomizes the Royce strategy.

RBA: A Classic Big Win in the Royce Style

The Ritchie brothers owned a furniture store in Kelowna, British Columbia, in the heart of that province's wilderness area, and in 1958 they found themselves in debt to the bank. They gathered some surplus sofas and chairs from the store and put them up for unreserved auction. When the auction had cleared their debt, they envisioned a business opportunity and went about scheduling more auctions. In 1963 they moved beyond furniture into unreserved auctions for used industrial equipment—tractors, loaders, backhoes, excavators, the stuff needed for construction, agriculture, mining, transportation, manufacturing, and forestry, and they sold $600,000 worth of goods. They expanded the business to the United States in 1970, and then further internationally toward the end of the 1980s. In 1998, the Ritchie Bros. gross exceeded $1 billion and management was ready to take the company public and engage the IPO process.

Royce analysts had been looking at the company for some time. It was a different kind of business, and, says Royce, "We are always alert to the offbeat and to quirky companies like this, and we were very intrigued from the start." They saw it as a niche business in a highly specialized field—a business that acts, in Royce's phrase, like "a toll business, collecting a fee each time you pass through." In such a business, more buyers mean more consignments of equipment to auction, and more consignments mean more buyers. Buyer and seller traffic feeds on itself, expanding the business, an enterprise that depends upon others to expend capital for the products offered—the goods they are seeking to sell. The auctioneers then collect a fee for overseeing the selling process. As the business builds, says Royce, "it creates a very wide moat for other businesses" to cross in order to compete.

When he speaks of a wide moat, Royce is referring to the first-mover advantage that in certain businesses establishes a significant barrier to entry for potential competitors to surmount. Ritchie Bros. had essentially invented a new enterprise, a market that had not existed before. No matter that they sort of stumbled upon it—a positive consequence of their financial misfortune. It was not quite the epiphany experienced by Sir Isaac Newton as he watched an apple fall to earth, but they knew what they had and took advantage of it. "Once it's established," as Royce puts it, "it's yours to screw up."

And Ritchie Bros. management, which now includes non-family members, has hardly screwed up. Their insistence on no-reserve auctions is evidence of their seriousness and integrity; they show high return on invested capital. As they have expanded they have exhibited the ability to take advantage of a cyclical downturn to add auction sites. Counterintuitive perhaps, but the used equipment business is recession resistant as financially secure buyers seek to take advantage of the more plentiful supply of product as it becomes available. Ritchie Bros. was looking like precisely the sort of small-cap company investment in which Royce specialized: undiscovered, non-mainstream, industrial, with high returns and high margins, and with a proprietary critical advantage for success. Honing it down until he was sure it was just the way he liked it, and assessing it on the Chuck Royce standard of potential acquisition—the if-we-owned-this-company standard—Royce bought Ritchie Bros. (RBA) on the Initial Public Offering and during the subsequent trading day at an average cost of $4.19. It was actually something of an unusual IPO, a financing mechanism usually used by companies much younger than the almost two-decade-old auction firm. But Royce still had not completely bought into the stock, wanting to see how Ritchie Bros. acted as a public company. And there was still a lot of analysis to be done. That "began the confidence-building process," as Royce says, and the firm continued to research Ritchie Bros.—its competition, customers, and process. Everything they found served to increase their confidence, and the Royce position in RBA grew in lockstep. As of this writing, Royce still has a position in the company.[9]

Royce management and RBA management meet "a couple of times a year." The former continue to be impressed with the latter. Royce analysts note the skill and savvy with which RBA handled the potentially tricky evolution to Internet bidding, which constitutes approximately a quarter of RBA's business. Return on invested capital remains strong, and Royce continues to believe the opportunity is huge for RBA to consistently grow market share. For Royce, one of RBA's largest shareholders, the result is "a compounding effect of a quality company that continues to do better" and that is pursuing an opportunity for even more growth. No wonder "we feel vindicated by RBA, by its progress as a company and a stock."

Finding the value in a small cap stock takes work, and building a bigger, more impactful position in a company you have invested in takes more work. But if it is work you have wanted to do since you were 15, then no matter your age, you are passionate about doing it. It is the kind of passion that keeps a person focused—acutely, intensely, relentlessly. The same guy who found his passion long ago while flipping through a loose-leaf binder, today powers on his iPad first thing in the morning to check the markets, still in love with the idea of stocks and the process of figuring odds. That is a life win, and it is a big one.

The Takeaway

EBIT—earnings before interest and taxes. EV—enterprise value. These are buzzwords for investment geeks but words, or rather, terms, to live by for Chuck Royce. Less complicated than it looks, the ratio EBIT-to-EV, EBIT/EV, is the single most important calculation he looks at in valuing a business. The best way to look at EBIT, albeit perhaps oversimplified, is as a proxy for cash flow. Enterprise value is the

(Continued)

market capitalization of a company (the share price multiplied by the total number of shares outstanding), plus the debt and preferred stock, less the cash and cash equivalents. Ignoring the premium to the market price that would be necessary to motivate a holder to sell his stock, this is the measure of what it would cost to buy the entire company. EBIT, as noted earlier, is essentially a measure of cash flow. Out of this comes a ratio that Royce, and many others, particularly value investors, regard as a truer, more consistent valuation technique than a price to earnings multiple. The measure used by Royce also touches on the balance sheet, since debt, to the extent it exists, is in the calculation along with the cost to service the debt, the interest payments. Adherence to rational cap rate[10] ratios is what attracts Royce to certain equities and what keeps him away from others. While Royce has tremendous respect for Amazon as a company, it is not a stock that he would own given that its cap rate is, approximately, a not particularly compelling 7 percent as of this writing with Amazon trading at $200 a share. Contrast this to Ritchie Bros.' significantly more conservative cap ratio of 15 percent, the preferred hurdle rate for inclusion into Royce's portfolio, when the stock was first purchased. However, this metric is not the only qualifying factor; the growth rate of EBIT is also a critical consideration, and Ritchie Bros. continues to experience growth that far outpaces the average company. When the cap ratio on a portfolio holding hits 5 to 6 percent, a valuation target that usually takes three to five years to reach, it will be sold. In fairness, Royce's valuation methods are not necessarily standard among small-cap investors, a number of whom do prefer to look at price-to-earnings multiples. Under that metric, Ritchie Bros. may not appear as attractive, an interesting paradox since Royce is, after all, a value investor. But the debate over what constitutes inexpensive is secondary to having a discipline and sticking with it, something that Royce clearly does. Thus, the ultimate take-away from this chapter is that, among the multiple ways to value a stock, Royce prefers to value it as a company, the way a potential financial buyer would look at it as an acquisition target; what return on investment would make the transaction work?[11] This analysis, part balance sheet, part income statement, sets a floor for protecting the investment, while the growth, or income analysis, provides the upside target. Although earnings can modulate up and down and be impacted by various one-time events, thus the issue with price-to-earnings, at the end of the day the assets are what survive. This is the point to take away.

Small cap investors must ensure that there are buyers willing to step in when they choose to exit a position, especially if the number of shares they own is disproportionately large to the average trading volume in the stock. The only way to have confidence that this will happen is if Royce sells while the story still has legs, so to speak. When Legg Mason acquired Royce Funds in 2001, its management clearly was hoping that the story still had some legs. That's why it paid a total of $215 million for the company under the assumption certain targets would be reached. Put in valuation terms similar to what Royce looks at, the purchase price was seven times EBITDA.[12] At the time Royce sold, his firm had $5.3 billion in assets under management (AUM). In the past 10 years, AUM have grown nearly eightfold. And while it can certainly be argued that Royce may have exited the position a bit too soon, it was this disciplined approach that allowed him to cash in. I did not ask him if he had regrets, knowing his answer would be "It was the right thing to do at that time."

Besides, no one has ever gone broke taking a profit.

Notes

1. Gregor Mendel was a nineteenth-century Austrian scientist and monk credited with being the founder of genetic science. He believed that certain genetic traits could skip a generation.

2. Investors in no-load funds do not incur a commission or sales charge since the funds are distributed directly by the fund manager rather than by a middleman.

3. In addition to companies such as S&P and Russell providing different market cap parameters for inclusion in their branded small cap indices, significant movement in the overall market averages will increase or decrease these levels to ensure that there is an appropriate universe of stocks to include.

4. Commonly called "benchmarks," active money managers are judged based upon how well they perform versus a particular index that is similar to their investment style.

5. www.russell.com/indexes/tools-resources/reconstitution/us-capitalization-ranges.asp. Figures as of October 2011.

6. www.standardandpoors.com/indices/sp-smallcap-600/en/us/?indexId=spusa-600-usduf–p-us-s–. Figures as of December 2011.

7. Interview with Consuelo Mack on *Wealth Track*, February 4, 2011.

8. There is no provision allowing for shorting stocks in the by-laws that govern the Royce Mutual Funds as is true for most all mutual funds.

9. Royce Funds may trade around a position, shaving the holding when it appreciates to a certain level that makes the holding less attractive than an allocation to other stocks. They may also sell it in its entirely and buy it back when the valuation again becomes attractive. In terms of Ritchie Bros., they did exceptionally well, realizing a profit of five times their initial investment, higher at some points, lower at others.

10. Capitalization rate, cap rate for short, is a technique for valuing a company in terms of what it returns on the investment. Cap rate is most commonly used in real estate for measuring how much income is generated on rental properties after various expenses, but Royce applies it to companies. Simplistically explained, cap rate as it relates to stocks is a measure of how much cash flow the company generates versus the price paid for its stock.

11. There are two basic types of acquirers of public companies: financial buyers, of which private equity firms dominate the category; and strategic buyers, companies that are looking to merge their operations into the company they are buying. Because there are more synergies and a greater

ability to reduce costs in a merger, strategic buyers can typically pay a higher price for an acquisition than a financial acquirer.

12. EBITDA, as with EBIT, is a conventional measure of a company's cash flow that is perhaps employed more often by financial analysts. A reason for this is that it takes into account the impact of depreciation and amortization of a company's assets. EBITDA: earnings before interest, taxes, depreciation, and Amortization.

Chapter 7

The Prophet of a Profitable Vision

A. Alfred Taubman

"I never look toward profits when I consider a development," says master developer Alfred Taubman. "I look to projects—to how qualified the project is. What can it do? What are its opportunities?"

Taubman may not look to profits—at least not immediate profits—but over a long career, he has amassed an extraordinary fortune through profitable investments in retail real estate development. It may be that the fortune was achieved precisely because of what Taubman saw when he looked to the "opportunities" of a project.

He certainly saw things others did not. Taubman virtually invented the enclosed shopping mall, now so intrinsic to American suburban life that it is almost a symbol of the country itself. And if he didn't invent the leveraged buyout, he nevertheless participated in what he thinks may have been one of the first on record, when he managed to persuade nine banks to lend him and his partners enough money—some $337.4 million—to buy the 77,000-acre Irvine Ranch, a premier real estate development in Newport Beach, California. He managed to do this because of what he saw when he looked at the Irvine project's qualifications and opportunities. Simply put, Alfred Taubman saw enormous possibilities, with the potential for even greater value: "$50 million of infrastructure already in the ground," he says, and "leases worth millions more." No wonder he was able to raise the money to buy the place—a big win, one of many big wins across a long career.

The profit came later, when he cashed out his stake, and it could have been even greater, Taubman says, if he had wanted to wait longer to cash out. "That would have been greedy," he says, "and I am never greedy."

Instead, he is innovative and excited by change. "Things always change," says Taubman. Famous for his attention to detail, he has built fountains and laid down terrazzo tiles in upscale malls, along the way to completely transforming the business of retailing by achieving significantly better productivity, as measured in sales per square foot, than anyone else in the mall business.

Along the way, the profits flowed, enough to create a fortune that *Forbes* estimates to be worth $2.5 billion.

Native Wolverine

Alfred Taubman was a child of the Depression. Born in 1924 in Detroit to immigrant parents, Taubman went to work in 1935 at the age of 11. A few years later, he had just started his freshman year at the University of Michigan—he is a loyal alumnus and formidable contributor—when World War II came along. Taubman enlisted and served in the Pacific.

When he came home, he went back to the university to study art and architecture, but the GI Bill was not quite enough to support

Taubman, a young family, and his studies, so he also went to work in an architectural firm.

Hundreds of thousands of others were doing much the same thing. Home from the war, they were marrying, starting families, beginning their careers, and moving out of the city into the suburbs to find more space and less concrete. To Taubman, this looked like future growth—demographically, economically, socially. And it prompted a question: Where would all these middle-class families shop once they had left the commercial downtown of the cities for the suburbs? The answer gave him a clue to a different kind of future value for the retail business, and for the infrastructure to support that business. What he saw in that future struck him as a key opportunity to ride the growth of strivers like him. "Demographically," he distinctively said, "I looked at the numbers, and as far as I was concerned we couldn't miss. And we didn't."

But it was not just demographics. Taubman had fresh ideas about how to design and build the real estate in which people shopped—ideas based on overcoming what he termed "threshold resistance," the physical and psychological reason that he said kept shoppers from entering a store or finding the right merchandise. Such barriers, Taubman argued, characterized the traditional retail store and the traditional retail experience, and he wanted to change both. Deep displays that confronted potential shoppers with a long, tunnel-like approach to the front door, that rarely attracted them with an appealing or imaginative appearance, and that took up valuable selling space struck him as both a physical and psychological barrier standing between a potential buyer and the seller's merchandise. He set out to design ways to overcome threshold resistance—to shorten the distance between display and door,[1] as he did for Apple's mall based retail stores, to encourage shoppers to step inside where a salesperson could begin the work of transferring confidence to a shopper, and where the excitement of making a purchase could be experienced.

No detail was too small for him to notice; no opportunity to enrich the shopping experience and increase the revenues of his tenants, and thus of his company, was ignored. Taubman regards himself as a merchandiser in addition to being a developer and landlord of retail space. An important part of retailing is presentation, and just as he had changed the storefront experience, Taubman essentially reinvented the layout of the mall. He was the first developer to take a truly innovative approach to floor plan design in each center. Instead of a bowling-alley approach of straight-line walkways, he built halls with edges and curves so that the storefronts stood out, and so that shoppers could see from a distance what lay ahead. This was good not only for the merchants who thereby drew the shoppers to their location, but also for those shops that customers passed along the way. Taubman even rethought the parking areas, making sure that shoppers had to pass through selling space on the way to and from their cars. The success of his tenants directly impacted his bottom line.

So in 1950, he began his own retail real estate development enterprise: The Taubman Company. His first assignment: Mrs. Ray's Bridal Salon in Detroit, a turnkey project that Taubman finished on time, on budget, and to great success for both Mrs. Ray and Mr. Taubman. He was on his way, and the successes kept on coming.

Big Wins: The Enclosed Mall and the Irvine Ranch

Taubman soon saw that retail real estate development was, in his words, "a numbers game," and as success followed success, the numbers prompted him to expand his horizons beyond Michigan. California was the obvious growth target, with its vast suburbs, its car culture, and its network of freeways. Indeed, the Golden State proved "fertile ground," as Taubman would later write, for his company. It was there, in the suburbs rising up in the Bay Area around San Francisco, that Alfred Taubman brought to fruition his concept of the super-sized enclosed suburban mall that offered much

the same scope and environment as the marketplaces found in traditional downtowns. It was there, too, that he polished his view that
he was really in the retail business, that a shopping center was a store
of stores, and that with the correct design they could break down
customers' threshold resistance. This strategy was the key to his
competitive advantage in "selling" the right stores.

Yet perhaps his most famous California venture was the purchase
of the Irvine Ranch, a premium planned community in famed
Orange County, that was already home to some of the state's—and
the nation's—wealthiest families. The opportunity arose when Joan
Smith, an Irvine granddaughter and family trustee of the foundation
that owned and administered the property, sued to halt the property's
sale to Mobil Oil Corporation, charging that the sale was for too
low a price and that the selling process was flawed. Smith won the
suit, and through friends of friends, sought out Taubman to see if he
would like to join in the submission of a new bid.

It was Charles Allen Jr. of Allen & Company who would actually
solicit Taubman's involvement in the project. Allen & Company is
not a household name the way Goldman Sachs and Morgan Stanley
are, but it is perhaps the most venerable and influential of the old-line
investment banks. Its clientele is dominated by a who's who of the
Forbes 400 and the corporations they represent. Each year, Allen &
Co. hosts an invitation-only conference in Sun Valley, Idaho that has
an extremely high bar for inclusion. Warren Buffett and Bill Gates
are perennial regulars, as are the CEOs of virtually every important
media and technology company in the world.

At Allen's behest, Taubman toured the Irvine Ranch, an area
almost five times the size of Manhattan. He then did his usual
appraisal. In his view, Mobil was prepared to operate the ranch as an
industrial business. Therefore, according to Taubman's assessment,
Mobil would apply a typical formula for acquiring an industrial
company that it believed would grow at about 10 to 12 percent annu-
ally, thereby boosting its own financial earnings. Most likely employing a price-to-earnings multiple on income generated by the Ranch,

Mobil made an offer of $24 per share. Well versed in the art of negotiating, Taubman knew Mobil could and would go higher than the initial bid.

So now Alfred Taubman had to assess how high he was willing to go and whether he would be able to bring along his investment partners or would have to go it alone. His partners were another A-list of the wealthy and accomplished. The list included Donald Bren, a well-established California real estate developer. Taubman hoped that Bren would bring in other local investors to ensure success in the acquisition of the property and in the ensuing development project, zoning approvals usually easier to come by when a local developer is involved. Looking "beyond earnings per share" as always, Taubman envisaged the opportunity in terms of the land value and the houses already on the ground—mansions worth $10 million to $12 million whose occupants were paying minuscule rents of $400 per month. A reappraisal found that those land leases were worth something more like $8,000 per month, and Taubman recalls with a smile how the Irvine residents staged black-tie banquets to raise money for lawyers to fight the new leases—an almost laughable initiative, since a number of these tenants were millionaires many times over—and forestall his acquisition of the property.

The effort, despite its elegance, failed. Where Mobil saw an industrial operation that might realize growth of 10 percent a year, Taubman saw it as a real estate deal with so much future value that while Mobil had bid low, he could outbid the oil giant's ultimately higher offers—at an initial bid of $27 per share—and still buy the ranch at a discount. "That's how I knew we could win," says Taubman, who was confident that Mobil would drop out; the oil giant was simply captive to a lack of imagination in valuing the asset.

That is exactly what happened.

"There's a pattern I know is successful in a project," says Taubman. "We may go into a deal that looks like it can return only 4 percent, but we know it'll be 20 or 50 percent. That's what I look for."

Conservative assumptions are often critical in preserving capital and ultimately driving return on investment.

The acquisition price for Irvine would eventually total close to $340 million. Taubman installed new management and changed the philosophy of the ownership to one that focused on operations, including development and profitability, rather than on passive rent collection. Six years later, Bren approached Taubman with an offer to purchase his shares and those of the friends he had brought with him into the transaction, valuing the Irvine Ranch at $1 billion. Taubman continued to envision more growth in the value of the Ranch but deferred to his friends' collective desire to sell at a large profit, adhering to his philosophy of not being greedy and of departing from the party accompanied by the people with whom he had come. He pocketed almost $150 million on the transaction, while the others divvied up approximately $200 million.

Core Competency

Alfred Taubman describes himself as a developer, not an investor. The term asserts a distinction, although perhaps not a big difference, between the two practices.

Traditional investors—in stocks, bonds, currencies, real estate—focus on a particular context or investment theme, develop ideas within that theme, then research each idea, analyzing it and weighing its risks and potential rewards. Developers do much the same, but the context in which ideas are found is always land and infrastructure. They research the idea up, down, and sideways, weighing risks and rewards. If the decision is to go forward with the development, they sink a lot of money into what they project will be an even greater future value. In a very real sense, every project is of course an investment.

The distinction, therefore, comes down to context. In Taubman's career, that means a single core competency—retail real estate development. Yes, he has dabbled in building other structures. When the mayor of Charleston, South Carolina, asked him to help save the downtown from a development stunningly out of keeping with that city's history and spirit by building a hotel, Taubman did so. "I did it because I thought it ought to be done," Taubman says. "This is a city important to America." He has also developed mixed-use urban complexes like the Town Center in Stamford, Connecticut, and Beverly Center in Los Angeles. And when a friend initiating a fund of funds asked Taubman to take a stake, he did so—"I wanted to help," he says. But the business of retail real estate development is what he knows and where he has a track record of extraordinary performance, having succeeded on 96 percent of his projects. "I haven't had many losers," says Taubman, "and I've covered the down-side pretty well." There seems little reason to depart from that very profitable home base.

That philosophy of covering the downside is something Taubman adheres to in his non-real-estate investing as well. Indeed, one of the key lessons to be learned from looking at Taubman's career is that, if and when you do venture out of your core business, spread the risk. Even when he has had the cash to put up all the equity—and that is most of the time—Taubman eschews taking on all the debt himself; instead, he brings in other investors. It is what he did when he bid for the Irvine Ranch in 1977, despite having the wherewithal to do the deal by himself, through his own assets and his relationship with various banks. This is a general principle that is critical to Taubman's thinking. It is also significant that Taubman is, in general, a long-term holder. That, too, is part of capitalizing on your core competency.

No wonder, that when he is asked to name his biggest win, Taubman answers without hesitation: "My best deal is The Taubman Company." He created it with a loan of $5,000 and he today owns "well over a billion dollars' worth of stock" that has provided a return of about 14 percent a year to its shareholders. "I'm a rich man," says Taubman. "The Taubman Company is how I got rich."

Check out the company's peerless portfolio and it's like scrolling through a who's who of the country's up-market malls. Indeed, researchers at Morgan Stanley, when preparing the underwriting for the company's IPO, found that Taubman malls are in more than 90 of the 100 highest-income U.S. zip codes. Today the company is also invested in "three very successful off-price malls." Says Taubman: "We do high end and low end. Never in between." (For a more detailed look at Alfred Taubman's malls, see Table 7.1.)

Table 7.1   Taubman's Malls

Operating Properties

Arizona Mills	Tempe, AZ
Beverly Center	Los Angeles, CA
Charleston Place	Charleston, SC
Cherry Creek	Denver, CO
Crystals at City Center	Las Vegas, NV
Dolphin Mall	Miami, FL
Fair Oaks Mall	Fairfax, VA
Fairlane Town Center	Dearborn, MI
Great Lakes Crossing Outlets	Auburn Hills, MI
International Plaza	Tampa, FL
MacArthur Center	Norfolk, VA
The Mall at Millenia	Orlando, FL
The Mall at Partridge Creek	Clinton Township, MI
The Mall at Short Hills	Short Hills, NJ
The Mall at Wellington Green	Palm Beach County, FL
Northlake Mall	Charlotte, NC
The Pier Shops at Caesars	Atlantic City, NJ
Regency Square	Richmond, VA
The Shops at Willow Bend	Plano, TX
Stamford Town Center	Stamford, CT

(Continued)

Table 7.1   (*Continued*)

Stony Point Fashion Park	Richmond, VA
Sunvalley Shopping Center	Concord, CA
Twelve Oaks Mall	Novi, MI
Waterside Shops	Naples, FL
Westfarms	Farmington, CT
Woodfield Shopping Center	Schaumburg, IL
Current Projects	
City Creek Center	Salt Lake City, UT
International Fin Center (IFC)	Seoul, South Korea
International Market Place	Waikiki, HI
The Mall at Oyster Bay	Oyster Bay, NY
North Atlanta Center	North Atlanta, GA
Plaza Internacional	San Juan, PR

SOURCE: Data from www.taubman.com, November 2011.

Taubman retired from any formal association with the company he founded, now known as Taubman Centers, although he is still involved by virtue of significant ownership of its shares and tight ties to its management; his two sons are today at the helm of the business. As would be expected, they still seek the master's counsel on occasion, but they have proven themselves to be strong stewards of the business, and visionaries as well, by opening a beachhead office in Asia and developing a project in Puerto Rico that will be consistent with the company's high-end venues.

Defeating Threshold Resistance

Taubman is not just about real estate, retail, malls, and money. His philanthropy is legion, and it derives from the same impulse that prompted him, as a young man with a background in both sales and design, to challenge the tried-and-true look of a retail shop.

Threshold resistance, in Taubman's view, is not limited to the world of retail. As he explains in his memoir, *Threshold Resistance: The Extraordinary Career of a Luxury Retailing Pioneer* (HarperBusiness, 2007), it also exists wherever people are stymied or held back from reaching their full potential. Taubman has used his fortune to help conquer this type of behavioral threshold resistance.

As the largest single donor to his alma mater, the University of Michigan, he has made major contributions to science and health research efforts there and elsewhere. He has also made extraordinary contributions to other universities, as evidenced by the Taubman Center for Public Policy at Brown University, the Taubman Center for State and Local Government at Harvard University, the A. Alfred Taubman Student Services Center at Lawrence Technological University in Southfield, Michigan, and the A. Alfred Taubman Center for Design Education at the College for Creative Studies in Detroit.

Higher learning is not the only lucky recipient of his largesse. Upon his recent discovery that 47 percent of adults in the city of Detroit, his hometown, are functionally illiterate, he was inspired to start at the very foundation of education by becoming involved in a new venture called Reading Works. This is only the latest in a long list of his philanthropic endeavors that he discusses with the same passion—perhaps with greater passion—than his having essentially discovered the modern mall. He writes in his blog, "It became clear to me that addressing the obstacle of rampant adult illiteracy is a logical, necessary step toward improving the economic and social prospects for Detroit's future. . . . With the proper training and support, an army of volunteers could have an immediate impact on this problem. Working one-on-one, we could turn this thing around one adult and one family at a time. And what a satisfying thing to do for the city you love."

Taubman once shot a hole-in-one on the Ocean Course on Kiawah Island and he is now doing what he can to make sure as many people as possible get *their* shot.

And by the way, it is not a coincidence that Apple chose Taubman malls as the location for many of their first retail stores. Given the extraordinary success of the Apple Store concept, the consumer found very little threshold resistance standing in the way of shopping for computers and iPhones within the environment Alfred Taubman perfected a half-century ago.

Art: A Raw Deal for Taubman

It was 1983 and the world discovered that artistic people have much more capacity for appreciation of a portrait than of a balance sheet. Sotheby's, the venerable British auction house, was in trouble and needed a lifeline. Having found no one in the kingdom of King Richard chivalrous enough to slay its financial dragon, Sotheby's came to America for a white knight and found one in master mall developer Alfred Taubman. The snooty art world turned up its nose, desiring perhaps someone more in line with its blueblood roots than some merchant from Detroit. But a merchant, a very wealthy merchant with very wealthy, art loving friends including Leslie Wexner, Henry Ford II and Milton Petrie (see sidebar: A Friend with Benefits), was what Sotheby's sorely needed—someone to restore excitement to the art world, to treat it as an experience, an attraction. In the spirit of the rich get richer, they would all profit handsomely when Sotheby's went public in 1988. The turnaround had required more than just cash; Taubman applied his retailing expertise to invigorate what had become a somewhat tired franchise by installing significant changes, such as luxury skyboxes above the auction floor.

The ultimate highlight for Sotheby's would be the auction of Jackie Kennedy Onassis's estate in 1996. Then the bottom fell out. The U.S. Justice Department had begun an investigation into price fixing between Sotheby's and its top rival,

Christie's. Taubman would step down from his post as Chairman in 2000 and was indicted in May 2001. His number two, Diane "DeDe" Brooks, was also indicted and faced a potential three years in jail. She would ultimately plead guilty and, in return for no jail time, agree to testify against Taubman. The indictment named others, but they all lived in England where price fixing was not a criminal offense. Ultimately, Taubman was convicted, agreed to contribute $156 million of his own money to the settlement, and spent nine months in a Federal prison hospital, a necessary concession to his then age of 78 and a heart condition. To this day, he maintains his innocence and calls into question the deal Brooks cut with the government, her motives being more than obvious. Having gotten to know Taubman and how he has lived his life and his charitable endeavors, I am going to line up on his side.

Close to the time Taubman was to report to prison, I was fortunate enough to be playing a round of golf at Deepdale Golf Club, a very exclusive course located about 25 minutes from New York City. The club has counted among its members Henry Kravis, Sean Connery, Tom Brokaw, and Pete Peterson, who arrived by helicopter as I was teeing off. Thirty-eight percent owned by Charles Allen's heirs from the investment bank, Allen & Company, Deepdale is a tremendous facility. Taubman was in the foursome in front of me and, knowing what he had just gone through and what he was facing, I admired his ability to keep the ball in the fairway. The world works in funny ways, and when I was finally introduced to Alfred, it would be at another exclusive golf course, Trump International in West Palm Beach. Nope—I am not a member there either, just America's guest.

The Process

For individual investors, the process Taubman uses to assess a potential development project is an invaluable template for assessing any type of investment opportunity. The process is shown in Figure 7.1.

It starts with looking at, again in Taubman's words, "how qualified the project is"—the opportunities for future value that it presents. That means exploring "beyond earnings per share," as Taubman puts it, and "appraising the value of the opportunity." In the world of retail real estate development, Taubman does so by assessing the land value and the "development upside." He looks hard at demographics within a 5-, 10-, and 20-mile radius of the project and he looks even harder at how the demographics are changing, because he knows they always do. He also knows—this is his core competency, after all—that where a shopping mall is concerned, "the indigenous population makes it profitable; the tourists are the upside." So he relies heavily upon the new science of psychographics—because this is also a man who keeps up with change—to understand the behavior and the tastes of customers and potential customers from data culled through social networks, search engines, and lifecycle forecasting.

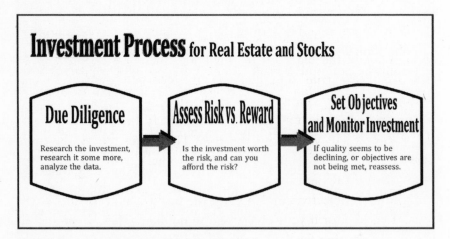

Figure 7.1 Taubman's Investment Process
SOURCE: Data from www.taubman.com, November 2011.

If a project passes muster and is seen to possess future value, the next step is to assess the risk—and cover it. Taubman concedes he has "a different perception of what risk means." As an entrepreneur, he sees doing nothing—"staying put," in his words—as risky too, perhaps more risky than going ahead. If that is the case and he assesses staying put as more risky than making a costly investment, he at least wants to spread the cost of that investment among partner investors.

The problem with having partners, however, is that it limits freedom of action. Taubman feels the same about his company having gone public in 1992. "I don't like being public," he says. "I like doing what I want to do." But when that is not possible, Taubman wants to be the one setting the objectives and managing the process. Design and cost standards must be met. "We cannot afford cost overruns," says Taubman. "We have to be right on costs." That means careful tracking of the project from beginning to end. Moreover, "We build good, solid stuff," he says, "and get credited for building elegantly." In other words, quality of design and execution are essential, especially since the investment is aimed at realizing returns over the long term. Says Taubman: "We build to last." He invests to last too.

How does this process translate into a guide for the individual investor who is buying equities listed on the stock exchange?

First, do the due diligence. If there is one thread that runs through all of the big wins in this book, it can be summed up in that seemingly trite sounding phrase. Research the investment, research it some more, and analyze the data.

Second, assess the risk versus the rewards. Is the investment worth the risk, and can you afford the risk? There must always be more upside than downside and the risks have to be heavily titled in favor of allocating time and capital.

Third, set objectives and monitor the investment. If quality seems to be declining, or if your objectives are not being met, reassess, even if you are investing for the long term—in fact, especially because you are investing for the long term.

A Friend with Benefits

Alfred A. Taubman is someone you want to befriend. He is fiercely loyal and unselfish, parceling out opportunities to others and does not forget those who have helped him along the way. He most certainly reaped the benefit of the relationships his old friend Henry Ford II had in Detroit and it was Milton Petrie, a billionaire retailer, who helped Taubman's company get its start and provided strong, effective counsel throughout the years.

He included his friends in the Irvine Ranch deal, both old—Petrie and Ford (by then no longer even a centimillionaire); and new—Donald Bren had communicated to Taubman that he could bring in other substantial investors. Although Taubman would ultimately pull together the financing through his own network of contacts, Bren was kept in the deal.

He is also great friends with Leslie Wexner, the founder of Limited Brands, Victoria's Secret, Bath and Body Works, and other retailing concepts. Wexner benefitted from Taubman's retailing expertise—and not only as a tenant. Taubman took Wexner on a helicopter tour of his Detroit malls and pointed out the Limited locations, castigating him for his stores being a "blight" on his luxury emporiums. Upon landing, Taubman used his architectural talents to craft a Styrofoam model of a more appropriate layout that would ultimately be the cornerstone for the design of the Limited stores.

While still a young entrepreneur and not yet the extraordinarily wealthy man he would become, Wexner called Taubman to congratulate him on the Irvine transaction. Eventually becoming close friends, they continued to do business over the years, Wexner's companies becoming important tenants in Taubman's malls. They would also partner on a number of investments including Taubman's acquisition of Sotheby's where Wexner would make a small fortune. It is good karma to share wealth and opportunity, particularly with similarly minded and resourced individuals. When Taubman purchased the New York office building that houses his personal office, Wexner rented three of the floors.

For all his commercial prowess and success, Taubman is relentless in his philanthropic endeavors by supporting numerous charities and blazing scientific trails in seeking a cure for some of the most deadly diseases. What he is most excited about at this point are the efforts he is funding in stem cell research. "We're curing breast cancer and Lou Gehrig's disease," he offers, the pride in his voice evident. Alfred Taubman was not making a forecast but rather a statement, and given his track record of success, I am a believer.

The Takeaway

The prophet of a profitable vision, A. Alfred Taubman has achieved a success that is rooted in an imagination that acutely sees opportunity that others have failed to envision. His imagination does not dip into fantasy; far from it. Rather, it is steeped in a thorough analysis of the base value of the property acquired, which limits the downside, and makes modest assumptions on the return. This is the takeaway for the average investor—a strategy that will be effective with most financial assets, be it a stock, bond, or real estate property: Buy a quality asset at the right price to limit your downside and assume modest upside in order to make the investment work. But the critical component to creation of Taubman's vast fortune has

(Continued)

been the vision of what could go right, really right, not as a result of happenstance or luck, but rather as a result of what he had envisioned that others had not.

How would this work for an average investor in the stock market? The first step is to find a company that is a sound business; one good example of this is a consumer product you come into contact with every day. Let's look at a couple of examples:

Next time you scarf down a quick sandwich and Coke, for instance, you might take note of Coca-Cola (KO). Certainly, this is a sound business. In fact, the market capitalization of the company is so large that significant gains in the stock price are unlikely. Additionally, the fundamental Coke thesis is well known, which means it would probably be difficult to discover a catalyst that would be sufficient to drive the share price substantially higher. In the case of Coke, therefore, your vision would be more of a view on the market, a difficult proposition in which to have incredible confidence. Bottom line on such an investment? Your downside would be protected by an above-average dividend yield, a strong balance sheet, and a non-cyclical business model. In the end, you may wind up with a stock that performs better during market declines but could lag on the upside.

But let's open our eyes to another company that is in a business we deal with every day, one where we tend not to think of its products as stock market investments. Take Qualcomm (QCOM), a company that offers a better example of applying the Taubman strategy to stocks. Best known for its wireless technology products and services, Qualcomm is not a commodity technology company like Dell, which manufactures computers by imbedding the technology of other companies (including Qualcomm), in its products. Rather, Qualcomm owns significant intellectual property (IP) in its own right; it is an innovator and has a substantial number of patents, licensing its technology to some of the world's top companies.

When I first looked at Qualcomm, I saw a company that bought back a significant amount of its stock, generated significant cash, had a strong balance sheet, boasted excellent management that owned a large amount of shares, and constituted a treasure trove of patents resulting from innovative technology. The company's growth in revenues and earnings was strong. The only thing that Qualcomm didn't have was any type of real relationship with Apple, the most exciting technology company in the world.

I knew I could buy Qualcomm stock at a price that was very fair, and I believed that over time, the shares would appreciate in value, returning a very nice gain on my original investment. But, I wondered, what could go really right? What could be the catalyst to drive shares higher than my expectations other than outperforming expectations on forecasted revenues and earnings or a new product cycle, standard fare for Qualcomm over the years? In one word, it was Apple. Were Qualcomm able to form a strong relationship with Apple, the growth would no doubt accelerate and translate into greater earnings. It made sense; after all, Qualcomm counted every other wireless product manufacturer among its customers.

And that is exactly what happened. Qualcomm first started doing significant business with Apple when its products were imbedded in the iPad 2 and then in the iPhone 4S. And the relationship continues to grow. Although not an avid stock market participant, Alfred Taubman, I think, would approve: A high-quality property with limited downside and enough that may go really right could change a return profile from good to incredible.

Note

1. Years later, when Apple was starting up its retail stores, a number of them in Taubman shopping center malls, Taubman's design staff helped Apple's store designers rethink their original design, suggesting what is now the stores' signature layout, including bringing the selling space right to the opening of the store, not set back to accommodate a reception-type area, as the Apple design originally had called for.

Chapter 8

The Twenty-First Century Belongs to China—and Commodities

James Beeland Rogers Jr.

J ames Beeland Rogers Jr.'s stature looms far larger than his person. He is not quite diminutive, but he is also not the prototypical master of the universe one might envision, with bulging muscles constrained by tights and a cape. The bow tie, crisp white shirt, gray suit pants held up with suspenders—braces in the more correct sartorial nomenclature—belie a near whirling dervish of activity. During our afternoon together, we coursed through midtown New York with a range of media pit stops along the way. It was a microcosm of who Jim Rogers is—someone always on the move, travelling the world under the rubric of adventure, yet always leaving with an investment thesis—newly formed or freshly ratified by what he has

153

seen, heard, experienced. He offers a sharp contrast to the universally held perception that Wall Street, a proxy term for the financial establishment, is a dull painting in black, white, and the occasional gray. In the facts of his background, in his achievements, in the courtly but pointed pronouncements with which he skewers some of the sacred cows of current economics, and above all in the way he goes about investing—like an explorer discovering and staking claim to new worlds—Rogers is one of the more colorful characters the Street has ever known.

This is the guy who grew up in Demopolis, an Alabama town so small the family's phone number was 5. It was in this small town that Rogers, a practicing capitalist from the age of five, began his business career gathering bottles and cans that fans had discarded in the stands at local baseball games. He would parlay his familiarity with the ballpark into a more profitable venture after he won the concession rights to sell peanuts and soft drinks at Little League games. By then, he was all of six years old. But being a concessionaire required capital, more capital than his bottle-collecting business had provided. So his father stepped in and lent young Jim $100—with the expectation that the loan would be repaid in full. It took a few years, but the elder Rogers would not be disappointed.

Although the culture in young Jim's section of Demopolis was somewhat homogeneous, all he had to do was venture to the other side of town—to what was, in then-segregated Alabama, the part of town to which the African-American population was restricted—to have his vision broadened, his assumptions challenged, his mind ignited. His mind not only on fire with awareness but burning with what he calls "delusions of grandeur," young Rogers won a Kiwanis scholarship to Yale. Going from the Deep South to the edge of New England confirmed for him that crossing borders "could teach me a lot about myself," so he next went even farther, earning a scholarship to Oxford University's venerable Balliol College. There, under more delusions of grandeur, he aimed not just to crew in the legendary

Oxford-Cambridge boat race, but actually to cox the Oxford team, a position not entirely dissimilar to quarterbacking a football team in terms of leadership skill required.

This was no ordinary water-borne drag race. The Oxford-Cambridge rowing contest, steeped in tradition dating back to 1829, is legendary enough to be known simply as "The Boat Race." Both universities are, of course, as English as Shakespeare and cold mutton and more ancient than both. Oxford, founded more than 900 years ago, is recognized as the first university in the English-speaking world, while Cambridge, a relative neophyte, opened its doors in the thirteenth century. In a country that prides itself on upholding tradition, Rogers's aspiration to cox the lead boat was made even more grandiosely radical by precedent; the only other American to cox the lead boat in the Battle of the Blues had succeeded not in crossing the finish line in first place, but rather in sinking the craft. Against the objections of many traditionalists at the university, but with the support of those that mattered most, Rogers assumed his position at the back of the boat and added a win to a lengthening list of accomplishments.

Between Yale and Oxford, Rogers had taken a summer job on Wall Street at Dominick & Dominick, one of the founding members of the New York Stock Exchange, and during that interlude he had fallen in love with investing. It seemed to him an enterprise in which, "If you could see the future and see what was going to happen and make an investment in it, you could make a lot of money." But a career would have to wait—duty called. As an opponent of the war in Vietnam, Rogers had no interest in serving in the armed forces, but he enlisted nonetheless. The motivation? To handicap the terms of his service. The Demopolis draft board was headed by a woman who had lost two sons in earlier wars and saw no reason why any able-bodied male should skirt his military obligations. So with a lottery number that made a tour in Vietnam likely, Rogers decided to enlist, which allowed him to choose the branch and location of his service. His education brought him the rank of lieutenant. His officer's duties allowed time for him to put money to work in the markets. He did so well that word spread, and it wasn't long before his commanding officer came looking for investment advice.

Wall Street was in trouble in the 1970s, experiencing the worst bear market since the Great Depression, and behind the scenes, computing technology was changing almost everything about the investment industry. It was a miserable time for anyone trying to make a living from the markets, but for those relatively new to the industry, as Rogers was, it was a period that would provide a great learning experience as well as an opportunity. After his discharge from the Army, Rogers found employment at Arnhold and S. Bleichroeder, which was then considered to be one of the investment industry's most highly regarded firms. One day in 1973, Rogers said good-bye to his day job and hooked up with a co-worker, whose upbringing was as different from his as vanilla to chocolate, to co-found the Quantum Fund. That colleague, George Soros, became a partner, and in a decade when the S&P had a cumulative increase of less than 47 percent, the two men managed their portfolio to an astounding 4,200 percent rise.

Needless to say, they each managed to accumulate a fortune— "more money than I ever thought I would have," says Rogers, which is why he simply figured he would "quit and have a new life." At the age of 37, that is exactly what he did—stepped away at a point when most people would not even have hit the halfway mark in their careers.

Easy Rider Explores the World

Rogers was much too busy to have ever been considered a "retiree," a word that conjures up an image of someone who spends his time in leisurely, rather than productive, pursuits. In fact, a reasonable observer would say that his exit from Quantum was nothing more than a change of venue and not an idling of effort. He still managed his own portfolio, and he lectured in finance at Columbia's Graduate School of Business while also sharing his investment wisdom on some of television's early financial talk shows.

By 1990, he was ready to cross more borders and explore more of the world. In fact, he set off to circumnavigate it—on a motor-cycle. His timing was pretty good, since beginning in the 1980s, two of the biggest chunks of the globe, the People's Republic of China and the Union of Soviet Socialist Republics, had begun to open their doors—at least on a limited basis to a limited number of outsid-ers. In China, Deng Xiaoping had earlier reaffirmed the Four Modernizations,[1] and the country was beginning to stir. Rogers managed to get permission to cross that vast nation, and he made a film about the experience. It was perhaps the film, he surmises, that encouraged the Soviet government to let him drive his motorcycle across Soviet territory. In any event, Rogers was able to include those two behemoth nations in his circumnavigation of six continents in more than 100,000 miles, all recounted in the book he wrote about his adventures, *Investment Biker*.

For Rogers, the adventure was not solely the ride itself, the places seen, the cities visited, the monuments and meals. Nor was it just the encounters, crises, occasional dangers, and close calls. "Had I been a football player," he says, "I'd have traveled the world looking for football games." But he is not a football player; he is a born investor, and he traveled the world *noticing*, if not overtly seeking out, investment possibilities.

Travel brought back to him the thrill of that first summer job on Wall Street—the sense of discovery that investing could provide. He felt it afresh as he thrashed his BMW bike across unfamiliar terrain and through exotic nations where all the sounds and smells were new to him. "If you come to a country and you see things that are going to be great in the country, my reaction was to go down-town and see if there was a stock exchange. And if there was, then I'd start making investments."

Explore. Get excited. Investigate. That just about summarizes the Jim Rogers formula of investing. His observations and instincts having always served him well; he sees no reason to disregard them. Nor, however, does Rogers rely solely on what those instincts and senses appear to be telling him. He checks the facts, and he brings a dose of skepticism to the task, sifting through numerous sources to assure himself of both the accuracy of the data he is looking at and the soundness of his own analysis. "Detail is the basic tool of anyone hoping to transcend conventional wisdom," says Rogers, asserting that he "will read any document I can get my hands on" to add a fresh perspective or flesh out an investigation.

The search is not limited to standard investment documentation. Rogers is a keen reader, analyst—and critic—of journalism, and he has seen journalism change markedly over the decades. He knows how to double-check a reference and determine which sources to rely on in his reading. He is also a student of history, a respecter of precedents, and a keen follower of the recurrence of trends. It is one reason he is, in his own words, "always in search of what is 'bearish.'" To him, the investment possibilities others have no interest in are the places to look for good deals.

All of it—history, current events, the facts disclosed, the possibilities dismissed by others—figure into the assessments that underlie Rogers's investment judgment and his ultimate investing decisions. The motorcycle circumnavigation didn't just give Rogers the time of his life and enough adventure for a book; it also helped enrich his portfolio. And, despite being held captive in the Congo for nine days,[2] it whetted his appetite for more travel and further investment discoveries. "I wanted to do it again," he says, "this time by car, and on a longer and even better trip." He planned that trip to be a millennium adventure, and brought along his then fiancée and now wife, Paige Parker. They set off in 1999 and covered 152,000 miles, passing through 15 war zones, sometimes having to grease their way through innumerable situations with just as many innumerable bribes. The trip inspired another book, *Adventure Capitalist*, and a lot more investments. Then, in 2003, Jim and Paige Rogers welcomed the first of their two daughters, and everything changed. It was, says Rogers, the beginning of the very best adventure of his life—fatherhood. It was also, Rogers told me when queried, his best investment and accomplishment.

But being a parent is different from being an investor. Children have to be nurtured and loved, two things that have no place in the black-and-white world of buying financial assets for profit. This period was thus a rebirth of sorts for Rogers, a man prone to picking up and travelling wherever and whenever he liked. Yet even more than experiencing a lifestyle change, Rogers sought to anchor his family's future to the economic story of the future.

A Father's Gift

Explorers and investors alike are future-focused—explorers because they always want to go one step farther, beyond the next mountain, and investors because the future is quite simply what they are betting on and where they will realize their rewards. Jim Rogers, explorer par excellence and natural-born investor, thus has a double dose of future fixation. Yet it may be fair to say that fatherhood concentrated his mind even more enthusiastically on what lies ahead, for the future is where his children will live, and, as with all parents, the children's future happiness and success are of paramount importance to Jim Rogers.

It is why Rogers penned his fifth book, *A Gift to My Children: A Father's Lessons for Life and Investing*, which is a compendium of the wisdom he accumulated over the years, in his many activities and across multiple travels.

It is also why, in a very real sense, fatherhood—and Rogers's fixation on his children's future—may be the source of his strengthened commitment to investing in China.

Bullish on China

In Chapter 4, you met another prominent investor, Jim Chanos, who shorted the construction boom China began to experience early in the twenty-first century and who has expressed doubts about the "growth model" for China and its future as an economic power.

Jim Rogers might agree with Chanos that the construction boom and its accompanying inflation must confront a "correction," but he has not an iota of uncertainty about China's future. If the nineteenth century was dominated by the British Empire, and the twentieth century was the American century, says Rogers, then the twenty-first century—without question in his view—belongs to China.

He sensed the potential of China as far back as that first trip in 1990, a time when conventional wisdom held that investing in China was a terrible idea because, in the unlikely event an investment there made money, the Communist government would simply confiscate it. Rogers was of a different mind. As he gunned his motorcycle across China's seemingly endless miles, from the rural countryside to the burgeoning city, everything that he saw and everyone he talked to filled him with a sense of that nation's potential.

If he had to characterize it all in one word, the word might be "discipline." Rogers saw people working from dawn to dusk, always seeking to improve, always ready to take another step forward for greater prosperity. He spoke to college students determined to build a better life than that of their parents and grandparents. He learned that China's 1 billion workers put one-third of their annual income into savings—more than 10 times the rate of savings in the United States. He observed that throughout China, people were studying English and Japanese, putting their effort where the money was.

Rogers knew that the Chinese had once been a people who seemed born to commerce and entrepreneurship, with an unexpressed instinct for capitalism, a knack for mercantile creativity, and a desire for great wealth and power. In 1990 he thought he saw those instincts being unleashed again, if only haltingly at first, after 400 years of repression, oppression, and decline. He came to believe that in China, "things are going to be great," and that the Chinese would soon reclaim their rightful place "among the best capitalists in the world." How could a country like this not grow? Rogers asked himself, and he answered by beginning to put his money there.

By 2007, with a four-year-old daughter and another on the way, he was ready to evidence his commitment even more dramatically. If the twenty-first was to be China's century, he wanted his children to have the advantage of growing up in the thick of it. He sold all his U.S. assets except for a few acres of land in Alabama and exited all U.S. securities in favor of a position in U.S. dollars—his only American investment exposure except for a negative bet against Citibank, homebuilders, and Fannie Mae in 2008—a prescient short that was a home run. Rogers also sold the New York City townhouse he, his wife and older child had lived in, and moved everything and everyone to Singapore.

Why Singapore? Rogers and his wife thought that mainland China itself might be a tad overwhelming and its environmental risks perhaps a bit tough for two young American children. Singapore offered a central and convenient location, a fairly cosmopolitan population, a reputation for order, fine schools, superb medical care, and a high level of efficiency in just about every endeavor of civic life. Above all, it was a place where his kids "could grow up speaking Mandarin," an achievement Rogers considered about the most important gift he could give them. "I will spend as much money as I need to," he has said, "to make sure my little girls go to Chinese schools, because the best skill I can give two people born in 2003 and 2008 is to know Asia and to speak Mandarin fluently. So far, this has turned out to be a great investment." His daughters are now fluent in Mandarin, no small accomplishment for such young children, and his oldest ranks among the top in her class at the school where classes are in English and Mandarin.

Ditto for his other investments in China—which cover just about everything *except* enterprises directly connected with the real estate construction boom, and which extend to the commodities the Chinese will require over the coming years to advance their return to being "among the best capitalists in the world."

The Commodities Connection

Jim Rogers doesn't appear to spend much time at home in Singapore. He's speaking at a dinner in New York, appearing at a conference in Shanghai, attending a meeting in Tokyo, participating in a forum in Seoul, giving a keynote address in San Francisco. The ultimate capitalist, he likes publicizing his comments, which increases the strength and reach of his brand.

The Jim Rogers you see on the screen is the same guy you meet in person. The man has a slightly mischievous twinkle in his eye, as if to let you know he is here to have fun, and he certainly seems to. Why shouldn't he? Jim Rogers today has capped untold material success with the total joy of a supremely happy family life. Debonair and voluble Rogers maintains the southern gentleman's gallant chivalry, but he combines it with the happy-go-lucky insouciance of a guy who says what he likes, when he likes, and where he likes, without feeling he has to mince his words or trim his convictions to this year's fashions.

And what he is convinced of today is that the world of finance "is about to be a disastrous place to put your money." Its moment has passed. "When I was at Yale and Oxford," says Rogers, "nobody wanted to go into the market. Now everybody does; Oxford guys are starting hedge funds in their dorm rooms. The U.S. produced 5,000 MBAs in 1958," Rogers goes on, "and there were none in the rest of the world. Now we produce 200,000, and the rest of the world does too." Result? "We're vastly over competitive. Financial institutions are under pressure from governments passing taxes and financial regulations to beat them down. And there is staggering global debt. So we're entering a period when finance will go into relative and then absolute decline." In fact, some may argue that this trend is already well under way.

What does it all mean? It means, says Jim Rogers, "The best job you can have in the next 30 years is to be a farmer." It means that it is once again the era of the producers of real goods. The long period when financial centers were the engine of the world economy is fading, as such a period has regularly faded during the course of history, in favor of a time when the centers that produce commodities will dominate economic power.

Rogers explains that currently the average age of an American farmer is 58—certainly on the back end of productive activity—while in Japan, huge agricultural fields sit empty because today's young Japanese adults have all headed to the cities to join the world of finance. "Things are so bad in Japan they're bringing in Chinese workers to farm the fields," Rogers reports. Clearly the need for young farmers in Japan—a country well known for its cultural coldness—is dire if they are willing to import citizens from China, a nation with whom their relations are not very cordial.

The need is made even more critical nearly everywhere in the world because, "By 2008, after 10 years of a bull market, people should have been bringing in new capacity—a new supply of commodities, but they didn't," Rogers says. Of these commodities—oil, iron ore, copper, metals, cement, food—Rogers points out that "The supplies that normally should have been coming online have not in fact come online." To Rogers, this signals that even if the *demand* for commodities flattens or declines, the fact that *supply* is declining means that prices will go through the roof. It means, in short, that, in Rogers's words, "The best financial investment going forward is commodities."

So commodities are what Jim Rogers is investing in.

And certainly, one of the key sources of demand for commodities in the coming decades will be China. Today, it uses one-tenth of the oil per capita that the United States does, but as its economy continues to grow, it will of course require more energy, more iron ore for industry, more cement for construction, more food as peasants increasingly leave the villages—and China's relatively small allotment of arable land—to head for the cities.

None of this, says Jim Rogers, is new. Economic eras alternate on a roller-coaster ride through history. As the old order in which he gained his big wins yields to a new order in which his children will have their chance, Rogers is investing in what he sees as their future—and in their ability to succeed in it.

The Takeaway

Jim Rogers is one of the top commodity investors in the world and has been for decades. Although mostly long commodities, he has also on occasion been short; he is by no means a "perma-bull," the standard colloquialism for someone always positive. So take him seriously when he says that China is the future and that commodities are a necessary part of that future.

Undoubtedly, Rogers would not feel as committed to his investment in China had he not spent significant time in the country, visiting both the major cities and those less populated. He told me that a critical part of his analysis is putting boots on the ground. After all, how can someone form an opinion on the prospects of an investment in an emerging market without actually experiencing the region? Economic press releases don't tell the entire story, Rogers would undoubtedly say, and part of the story simply is not enough for an investor. Sure, financial disclosures are allegedly thorough and government data releases supposedly accurate,* but

*Others, including Jim Chanos, would look at any government release with a skeptical eye. China is a managed society, so is it unreasonable to assume that they assiduously manage their data flow as they do most communications?

documents alone leave out the personality of the area, the palpable visuals that accompany the bustling activity. Relying on documents alone denies an investor the subtleties that can be inferred from interactions with local business people and ordinary individuals, conversations that let you in on how their lifestyle is changing and how they define their expectations of future needs and wants. Boots on the ground, when accompanied by a thorough review of pertinent documents, provide the truest picture of an economy.

Rogers puts forth a premise that is difficult to dispute. After all, how can anyone quibble with the age old truism that "seeing is believing?" But of course following Jim Rogers's dictum would take significant resources—far in excess of what's available to the average investor. On the other hand, not everyone believes that on-site visits are critical for thoroughly researching an investment thesis. Chuck Royce, also profiled in this book, prefers not to speak with the management team of a company he is researching because he believes that they cannot be entirely impartial. Perhaps even more pertinent, Jim Chanos has never been to China but is fully committed to his thesis to short the banks and property developers there. So who is right? Well, here is the good news for the average investor—all three are. Travel to China if you like or save the airfare and use the internet to do research. It is all there, whether in the CIA *World Factbook*, an excellent source of information, or in any other legitimate document. A certain threshold of due diligence is required to achieve appropriate confidence in your position so that fundamentals rather than price volatility dictate your holding period.

What exactly does Rogers see in China that has him so convinced that he uprooted his family? Here's the story. With nearly 1.4 billion people China has the largest population on

(Continued)

the planet. While it is still technically a Communist regime, very few regard it as such anymore, at least from an economic standpoint. According to the September 2011 tally by *Forbes*, China has 146 billionaires,[*] placing it second to the United States, albeit a distant second since the United States has more than 400[†]—but far ahead of most developed nations with a much longer tradition of capitalism. What would Mao Tse-Tung say about that? Underlying the sprouting of an upper class is China's burgeoning economy, which has grown at a rate of 8 to 10 percent, as measured by GDP, over the past couple of years. This is an astounding figure, especially considering that the Chinese economy is already the second largest in the world, having surpassed Japan in 2011. China's growth rate is, of course, even more incredible when you consider that almost everyone else was staring at a recession during the same time period. But will this hyper-growth rate continue? Rogers would offer a resounding *yes,* while acknowledging there will be recurring setbacks along the way just as there were in the United States as our economy grew. Imagining the Chinese populace as poor farmers in tattered clothing and sandals is a mistake. The increase in household wealth, resulting from the migration of huge numbers of people from rural areas to the cities, has led to an incredible and unprecedented construction boom. The continuing increase in consumption of all goods leads to the question of affordability. How can a country that ranks 125th in GDP per capita pay for all this growth? No problem. China has more cash and less debt than any other country.

So there it is in a nutshell. As China grows, it will consume more oil, more goods, more food—more of every-

---

[*]www.forbes.com/sites/russellflannery/2011/09/21/u-s-vs-china-rich-lists-america-is-still-winning-for-now/.
[†]Ibid.

thing. And China is not the only country of size that is in an über-growth stage and in need of more resources. India is right behind it, both in population and in need, and not far behind India, is Russia. Meanwhile, the developed countries of the world—the United States, Japan, Germany, France, Italy, and so on, despite slower growth, have not experienced a lessening of demand for commodities of all types.

This, then, is the absolute takeaway and the investment thesis Jim Rogers is banking on. Commodities are in limited supply, yet there are more countries and more people driving consumption. China has taken a long-term view and has stolen a march on other countries. For example, China's oil consumption is growing at an alarmingly high rate, from 9.07 million barrels a day in 2010 to an estimated 10.13 million barrels a day in 2012, according to a report by the International Energy Agency (IEA).* It has therefore locked up a significant and permanent supply of crude oil by making investments in many energy entities around the world in exchange for a percentage of those companies' production. According to the IEA,[†] in 2008, China spent $18.2 billion on acquisitions of energy properties, only to significantly surpass that total in 2009 at $29.4 billion. Acquisitions continued on a similar pace in 2010 and 2011, although figures were not available as of this writing. These transactions take multiple forms including a loan against production, the acquisition of a leasehold interest or the outright purchase of a company. Regardless of the structure, they all have the same effect, which is to shrink the amount of energy assets available to other countries, thus tightening supply and driving prices higher.

*http://omrpublic.iea.org/currentissues/full.pdf.
[†]www.iea.org/papers/2011/overseas_china.pdf.

(Continued)

This is what Jim Rogers is wagering on—unprecedented global growth driven by emerging economies such as China and India. Did it take boots on the ground to realize this is happening? No, not really, but it helped. Can individual investors feel comfortable making the same investment as Rogers? They can, depending upon their time frame and tolerance for volatility. Commodities are Rogers's financial instruments of choice for expressing his bullish view on China's growth prospects. This is not a bad way to go, for although the boom continued booming through 2011, China's stock market declined by more than 20 percent during the same period of time. Nonetheless, most investors don't possess the appetite for direct investment in commodities given the aforementioned high volatility and potential for loss. Keep in mind that no investment case, no matter how logical and seemingly foolproof, is without risk. As of this writing, Rogers's present portfolio of long commodities and currencies is hedged by shorts in U.S. technology, emerging markets stocks, and European shares. Given his long-term view, I do not expect much change in the portfolio for quite some time.

If you are an individual investor unfamiliar with commodity markets, perhaps the best way to participate in the commodity boom is through certain equities traded on exchanges around the globe. For example, among U.S.-listed equities, the obvious stocks to consider include: manufacturers of construction and mining machinery, such as Caterpillar, Inc. (CAT); producers of crop fertilizer including Potash (POT),★ Agrium (AGU), and Mosaic (MOS); the multitude of energy companies that benefit from rising oil prices,

---

★A state-owned Chinese company had expressed interest in acquiring Potash Corporation of Saskatchewan but withdrew under political pressure from the local government in Saskatchewan, Canada, where 25 percent of the world's potash supply is produced.

including the likes of Exxon Mobil (XOM) or Chevron (CVX). However, keep in mind that these companies are not a pure play on commodities; their business interests are tied to many factors, global economic growth being only one, albeit a most important variable. Additionally, there are a number of exchange-traded funds (ETFs) and exchange-traded notes (ETNs) that more acutely track the direction of certain commodities including silver, gold, and grains. None of the aforementioned investments are recommendations, since risk tolerance is an individual decision. As always, do your own work, listen to your own trusted advisor, or invest with a professional.

Notes

1. Deng is credited with officially presenting The Four Modernizations—agriculture, science and technology, industry, and military—during a speech in December 1978. This could be regarded as the beginning of reform in China.
2. Rogers was released, unharmed, without having to pay a ransom, but both he and his captors thought it best that he leave the country as soon as possible.

Chapter 9

Opportunity Is Where You Find It

R. Donahue Peebles

D on Peebles is a big man with ambitions and a track record of achievements to match his stature. He set out to be a millionaire by the time he was 30 and beat his own goal by three years. He took his talents to Florida and helped reinvent the spirit as well as the look of Miami Beach. The Peebles Corporation, the country's largest African American real estate development company, with a multibillion-dollar national portfolio, is comprised of office buildings, hotels, residential developments, and mixed-use complexes in cities across the country—all notable, as Peebles intended, for "something more than bricks and mortar." In real estate parlance, they are Class A properties.

Get ready, New York. Don Peebles has arrived, he is primed to capitalize on what he sees as the city's "unique creativity and ingenuity," and he is eager to do business.

He does not come unprepared or unconnected. A long-time summer resident of the fabled Hamptons on Long Island, Peebles has widespread relationships among the business and political movers and shakers who can help make things happen in New York or any other market. He is himself a player in national and local philanthropic efforts and has been a formidable political fundraiser for the likes of Presidents Clinton and Obama, to name just two.

But this is a man who grew up with, as he says, no sense of "limitations or impediments" to what he could achieve, and New York, as the biggest stage of all, offers even more room in which Don Peebles can stretch his dreams and test his mettle.

No Limitations

His is not a rags-to-riches story. The riches did eventually materialize, but Peebles never knew rags. His parents divorced when he was five, leaving his working mother to raise him. His father, a U.S. government file clerk who also worked as an auto mechanic on weekends, was unable to meaningfully contribute financially to his upbringing aside from monthly child support payments and inclusion on his government-provided medical plan; nevertheless, raw poverty was not his experience. His mother, however, most certainly struggled to make ends meet. From observing his parents' experience, he learned a great deal about how tough it is to make a living and how dispiriting economic insecurity can be. Peebles watched his mother labor as a secretary during the day while attending night school in pursuit of a real estate license. After they moved to Detroit to be closer to family, he witnessed her success in real estate but unfortunately it was not long lived for when they relocated back to Washington, D.C., she would again struggle for work. The ups and the downs were not lost on him.

Both parents were intelligent and, according to Peebles, "entrepreneurial." They worked very hard, but their efforts alone were not quite enough for the kind of reach-as-far-as-you-can wealth Peebles knew was out there, waiting to be seized and enjoyed. He understood that a mother's sole responsibility to raise and support a child was a very limiting factor in terms of the risk one can assume in an attempt to shoot for the stars. At the age of 17, he vowed to himself that without these constraints, he would seek and obtain the financial means that would guarantee that everything was possible, with no more struggle, no more worry. The opportunity was out there, somewhere, the only question in his mind being not if, but how.

There was never any question in his mind that he could do so. He was brought up to believe there were no boundaries or impediments to advancement, and he saw that reality demonstrated around him. His grandfather had always told him, "In America, there are no limitations on what you can do." How this belief lodged itself in an African American man born and raised in the segregated South, who worked his entire life as a doorman at a Sheraton hotel[1] in Washington, remains unexplained. But it is also true that this doorman managed to send four of his five daughters to college, and he lived to see all of them become either professionals or the wives of professionals.

Peebles himself, born in 1960, was a boy during the height of civil rights activism and came of age at the start of an era of almost galloping opportunity. Politically active from boyhood, son of a politically engaged mother, Don Peebles at 16 became a U.S. Capitol page, then an intern for California Congressman Ron Dellums and a staff aide to Michigan's John Conyers. If role models were needed, he had before him on the floor of the House of Representatives a cadre of African American men of great stature flexing their substantial political muscle, not just to ensure this new era of opportunity but to be heard on all the questions of the day. And there were a significant number of important issues back then, including the aftermath of the Vietnam War and the signing of the Nuclear Non-Proliferation Treaty. This was heady stuff and "it raised the bar," Peebles says of the experience now. And it taught young Don about

"the power of relationships and how they make politics work"—
an essential education for the future. He would prove to be an excellent student.

In fact, this education, "up close and personal," as Peebles says,
in power and the way the world works was so comprehensive and
profound that he left college after one year as a pre-med student at
Rutgers. He came home to D.C. and in effect apprenticed himself
to his mother, who by this time was running a small real estate
appraisal business. In those days, Peebles recalls, the appraisal business
was loosely regulated, and apprenticeship was a standard way to gain
the needed expertise, which Peebles did, eventually going solo. He
had also begun selling real estate in 1979 after becoming a licensed
agent. So in a sense, the pieces were all in place for him to turbo-
charge a career toward his goal of becoming a millionaire by the age
of 30—except for one essential piece of the package: politics.

Unlike the appraisal business, real estate investing was a highly
regulated industry. It is also, as Don Peebles has pointed out to more
than one interviewer, a "regional business . . . driven primarily by
regional economics and regional land-use guidelines."[2] For these
reasons, doing the business right requires frequent interaction with
agencies of government and the people who can get things done in
those agencies. That's politics, and that was where Don Peebles knew
he needed to go next.

The year was 1982. After a first term highlighted by significant achievements in efficient governance but diminished by a
rising crime rate and some mini-scandals in his administration,
Washington Mayor Marion Barry was running for reelection and
faced three challengers in the primary. The establishment choice was
Patricia Harris, a sophisticated, urbane lawyer and public servant
with impeccable credentials—most recently, as a member of Jimmy
Carter's cabinet.

Peebles didn't know Mayor Barry particularly well prior to the
campaign, but as his involvement grew they built a warm relationship. In addition to believing Barry was the right person for the job,

Peebles saw an opportunity to immerse himself in local politics, an association that could help his real estate business. He threw his lot in with Barry, organizing and sponsoring fundraising events as he built a friendship with the candidate. But he showed his inherent political savvy with the fundraiser breakfast he scheduled for two days *after* the primary–a brilliant tactical move for an experienced politician, but all the more impressive for a 22-year-old new on the scene. As Peebles had sensed would happen, Barry won the primary in a landslide with 59 percent of the vote, and as Peebles also surmised, that meant that one-time Harris supporters in the business community would be chomping at the bit to get to the Barry breakfast and mend fences with the city administration. That's exactly what transpired. The $500-a-plate breakfast was standing room only, and it was Don Peebles who introduced Candidate Barry to the packed house of business and community leaders.

The payoff came quickly. Peebles was appointed to the city's property tax appeal board, which hears appeals from commercial property owners disputing their annual tax assessments, and he became chairman a year later. He implemented a series of reforms that vastly improved the way the board worked, thereby simultaneously polishing the image of the man at the top, Mayor Barry, as Peebles had intended.[3] At the same time, he continued his appraisal work, having formed his own appraisal business in 1983. No question: the connections Peebles made through this work and the insight into real estate helped ensure him a steady flow of clients and an ever more lucrative payday. He may have left college after only one year, but he was certainly a great student of the real estate business and of politics.

He was doing well in both when, in 1986, a real estate broker came to him with a possible deal—a project to develop a new commercial building in Anacostia, an historic but neglected section of D.C. where no new commercial properties had been built in decades. The bid-offer discrepancy between buyer and seller was substantial—$750,000 offered against $900,000 asked—when the broker approached Peebles, hoping he would rescue the deal and his commission. Peebles saw opportunity and decided it was time to become a principal rather than continue to be just a facilitator; he met the seller's price. It was not a bid made in haste by someone seeking to own his first significant property; despite his age, Don Peebles was already a seasoned veteran when it came to understanding property values. And it turned out that he had properly assessed the potential for the property, being reasonably certain that the government had an appetite for office space in an area that cried out for redevelopment, an initiative Mayor Barry certainly backed and for which he has justifiably received substantial credit.

By the time the transaction closed, Peebles had made believers out of others who would provide the necessary capital, mitigating his risk and leaving him with 50 percent ownership. His contribution to the partnership was ultimately limited to finding the opportunity, raising the financing, and crafting the transaction. Today, he still has his ownership interest in the property, in which the government continues as a tenant, providing Peebles with a nice annuity each year in the form of rent.

So that first deal, development of a Class A office building at 2100 Martin Luther King Avenue, SE, laid the groundwork for where Peebles is today. It encapsulated the formula that would be his signature for future deals: the seller's price, as long as it is fair and reasonable; his terms; other people's money. It was in this deal that he also confirmed his ability to play politics and the importance of doing so. It was here he learned that, in his words, "The most important thing in a deal is finding the deal. You can get anybody to execute, but doing the deal is what's special." Putting it all together, the Anacostia development would provide the framework for all the deals Peebles would do going forward—find and assess the opportunity, assemble the financing, work through the difficulties that had kept other developers at bay, and bring the project to profitable completion.

On paper, Peebles was now a multimillionaire, a few weeks after he celebrated his twenty-seventh birthday. Perhaps even more important than the wealth he had accumulated was the repeatable process that he could now apply to future transactions. He has shown that he possesses the most important qualities for achieving his goals—the vision to discern an opportunity that others with more experience had failed to see, and the can-do attitude to get it done. He had seen, through the eyes of his family, that barriers are self-constructed and thus either did not exist in practical terms or could be overcome with determination and a plan. Over the next three years, he acquired more properties, opened a tax assessment appeals business, paid off his debts, and bought a million-dollar house on Embassy Row. At the age of 29, he was, in his words, "at a different level."

The level would keep rising. As Peebles sought more projects and better ways to navigate the intersection of real estate and politics, he stepped up his game. He made friendships on a national level, and in 1992 he was with Bill Clinton in Arkansas on election night, and is currently a financial supporter of Barack Obama. He has also provided advice to President Obama's administration.

Finding the Deal

Don Peebles strives to be involved in what he calls "transformational projects." He is an unabashed capitalist who is in business to make as much money as possible, and his first consideration on any project is the potential profit. But having achieved a significant amount of success and stature, both in real estate and as an extremely wealthy, well-connected businessman, not just any project will garner his interest. "I want to be engaged," he says. "I am attracted to signature projects, projects that are intriguing and that will have some symbolism beyond bricks and mortar." He articulates that through The Peebles Corporation. Its portfolio embodies his vision; he is, as he says, "the architect of the marketing of this vision." So only those projects that resonate with Peebles are likely to make it into the portfolio.

It is why every project is a fresh start and why he always feels like an entrepreneur. As opposed to the kind of business in which an individual can succeed by having one good idea and repeating it over and over for years, or the kind of business an individual perhaps has inherited and is simply trying to preserve by not rocking any boats, real estate development as Don Peebles practices it means building a new business with every project.

And that, of course, is why he wants a project to have meaning beyond dollars and cents. Whatever it is, it is going to require risk, time, and effort, and if Peebles is going to commit to all of that, he wants to feel engaged. So he prefers that a project either be socially transforming or that it be of exceptional architectural or design quality—or, preferably, that it be both. And, of course, each project becomes an advertisement for the next one—for zoning boards in other cities to regard with admiration, hoping to replicate that success within their borders; for potential investors to marvel at the cash that is thrown off and increases in value; and for sellers who want to get a deal done with someone who can execute.

Peebles spent several more years combining politics and business in D.C. He remained close to Mayor Barry—at least until Barry backed out of a deal Peebles had been counting on.[4] Eventually though, he felt he had done what he wanted to do in his hometown; he knew the players, knew the business landscape, knew the politics. Washington, the world's largest political stage, had become too small for Peebles in terms of new projects to find and develop; he felt hobbled in his desire to spread his efforts in a new direction. It was time for a change. He and his wife, Katrina, and their then infant son, had vacationed in Miami in 1995 and had liked the place. But more than just kicking back and enjoying the warmer southern climate and the renaissance of South Beach, Peebles saw opportunity. It certainly makes sense that a person who achieves millionaire status in his mid-twenties from a standing start, three years ahead of his own aggressive schedule, would always be looking for what is next. Über-successful people don't suffer much downtime, and Peebles is no exception. He put good leisure time to work, taking a tour of Miami beachfront real estate and noting what the papers had to say about development projects. This seemingly inconsequential decision would shape the next decade and a half of his professional life, providing the signature projects that would add substantially to his net worth and reputation. It would also shape his business and family life, since he decided to move both to Miami Beach.

On the Beach

Peebles's first win in Florida—indeed, the property that intrigued him when he first heard about it during the vacation with his family—was the Royal Palm Hotel project, as politically complex as a project could be, set against a background of ethnic and racial divisions and south Florida's unpleasant racial history. The city of Miami Beach owned the old hotel, which, although dilapidated, had been certified by the city's engineers as structurally sound, and it had been set aside for an African American developer. The set-aside was part of the price for ending the African American tourism boycott of the city that had followed the city's snub of Nelson Mandela. That snub had been in response to the large Cuban-American population's anger over Mandela's positive remarks about then-Cuban President Fidel Castro. In a city that had been segregated until the 1960s, and whose disparate ethnic populations lived warily together, such stitched-together agreements were a way of life—or at least of politics.

What Peebles learned about the Royal Palm was actually from a *Miami Herald* article not so much about the old hotel as about the soaring value of its neighbor, the Shorecrest Motel. Peebles then presciently purchased the Shorecrest, and when the city officially put the Royal Palm up for development, it did so on the condition that the Shorecrest also be developed. The bidding process was long, drawn out, and almost surely loaded in favor of the major hotel chains that had partnered with African Americans to meet the set-aside requirement. Peebles wanted in, but if he won he had no interest in being the face for someone else's deals, which would have been an easier but less fulfilling and less lucrative path. He was every bit as good a developer as anyone else, and he wanted it to be his own project.

Peebles dove into Miami politics and into the Miami public opinion arena to make his case. Control of the Shorecrest effectively washed out his risk; he could sell the property at a handsome profit and walk away if he did not win the bid. It was a good insurance policy, since the Shorecrest was a necessary component to any development deal. Although it did not show in the fierce competition for the property, some developers were wary of bidding on the Royal Palm since potential buyers were not permitted to inspect the property, which is normally the custom. The city did not care about established practice, so the Royal Palm was being offered in "as is" condition. But winning the bid was what Peebles was there for. Especially because it marked his foray into south Florida, he wanted to send a clear message that he was not going away and that he could deliver. He wanted the African American community to understand that, and he wanted the city fathers of Miami Beach to understand it. In time, they did, and he won the bid and took possession of the Royal Palm.

Of course, the building was not, as he had been assured, structurally sound; in fact, it was eventually condemned and had to be demolished. Historic preservation issues then came to the fore. It all added to the cost of the project, expenses he did not anticipate, and the financial pressure mounted. The schedule slipped. Peebles weathered it all. From the marriage of business and politics, it is probably safe to say, the resulting progeny is often aggravation, the kind of aggravation that people think should make you want to flee the contest. Not Peebles. He understands that this is all part of the business. The new Royal Palm Hotel opened in 2002 in the heart of South Beach—a beachhead, so to speak, for Pebbles future wins.

In fact, over the course of those 13 years while based in Miami, plus two additional years commuting from Washington, Peebles undertook some of his most significant and best-known projects. He also refined the process that has become his signature as much as any of the buildings he develops.

The Peebles Way to a Win

The process starts with an assessment of how much can be earned if the project is done well, and how well the project has to do to achieve that dollar figure. Armed with that assessment, Peebles can quantify the risk he might have to take so that he can mitigate the downside. He is, he says, a "calculated risk-taker, not a big risk-taker."

To that end, he does not eschew leverage. "If you're creating wealth, leverage is your best friend," says Peebles—that is, "nonrecourse leverage. Leverage with recourse is what gets people into trouble."

To make the reward/risk assessment, Peebles first identifies the market segment that may be attracted to the particular project. After he understands who they are, he finds out their current and projected economic conditions. The next step is determining what type of project he needs to build in order to win that clientele, who may be competing against him for the same customers, and how he stacks up against them. "I need a very significant competitive advantage" to undertake a project," says Peebles. "If not, I pass on it."

In Miami, most of the development during the 1990s was, like the Royal Palm, in South Beach, but as that decade drew to a close, Peebles had his eye on a property closer to North Beach. It was the once venerable, now down-at-the-heels Bath Club on Millionaires Row, founded in 1926 as a private WASP enclave to which neither

Jews nor African Americans were admitted. Peebles became its first African American member in 1996 and took ownership of the property in 1999, the same year the Bath Club had elected its first Jewish President. This confluence of events was likely not in the plans of the founding WASPs.

He saw *his* Bath Club as a residence tower with sufficient acreage for some special amenities. But he knew he was aiming at a very high-end market segment, the kind of people, he judged, who were attracted to Fisher Island, the barrier island three miles off the Florida mainland that is said to have the highest per capita income of any location in the United States. Fisher is home to people who prize and can afford a distinctive level of privacy, plus open space, top-of-the-line amenities, and low density that engenders a kind of tribal collegiality. Peebles's intention was to offer all that without the ferry ride.

Using himself as the measure of the client, Peebles asked himself what he would want in a vacation apartment. The answer was that he would want the same things he can find at home: significant square footage and an absolute sense of privacy—attributes hard to come by in Miami Beach apartment buildings. His vision, therefore, was for the residences of the Bath Club to offer potential buyers two significant advantages that other developments could not provide: a very substantial unit size combined with a large amount of space to create a gated and private enclave (tribal collegiality plus amenities). Add in his high-quality, signature architecture and the project was as can't-miss as a real estate project can be.

But the risk was significant. A referendum had just passed freezing all zoning and thus significantly limiting the possibilities for redevelopment of the property.[5] However, with this issue hanging over the already beleaguered owners, they now had an even greater motivation to sell as quickly as possible. Motivated sellers are a developer's best friend, but this was not a straightforward situation where a buyer could just swoop in and know that his downside was protected by a fire sale price since the zoning changes added a significant element of risk to the purchase. But if Peebles wanted in, this would be his best opportunity and he would have to put his money at risk without delay, not knowing with certainty that he could build the project he envisioned. Being risk conscious, if not risk averse, he obviously wanted to mitigate his potential downside—and he wanted to know ahead of time that it could be mitigated. He rolled up his sleeves and worked with his team of lawyers to find a solution. Their joint efforts yielded a legal loophole that could make it possible for the city commissioners to effect a change in zoning category. This essentially meant the project would hinge upon a political solution, a playing field Peebles knew well, one on which he was comfortable and in which he had experienced significant success. He went to work. His worst-case scenario, as he saw it, was that he could sell the property and not develop it himself; best case, if he could obtain the zoning change, was to "build a signature building and have it on my track record." He sought out meetings with each of the commissioners who held the decision power to transition Peebles's plans into reality—his first foray into luxury residential development. Don Peebles understands what motivates politicians to do what is sometimes anathema to them, to make a relatively quick decision for the right reasons. He persuaded five of the seven commissioners to back him, convincing them that a high-end residential property was in the best interests of the community. At this point, knowing the outcome and having mitigated the risk, he put up the cash and took control of the site.

The Bath Club tower became precisely the success he had envisaged. See more on Peebles's successes in Table 9.1.

This is the process Don Peebles has brought with him to New York. In his eyes, New York City is "the greatest real estate market in the world" and "capitalism at its best." He intends to build transformational projects here too. Just as the Royal Palm "helped bring Miami back," as he says, just as his first project in Anacostia helped reinvigorate a neighborhood in Washington, Peebles is looking for "more than dollars and cents" in the Big Apple. It is the place, he

Table 9.1 Key Projects

Complete

The Residences at the Bath Club	Miami Beach
The Royal Palm Hotel South Beach	Miami Beach
Courtyard by Marriott Convention Center	Washington, D.C.
The Lincoln	Miami Beach
10 G Street, N.E.	Washington, D.C.
2100 Martin Luther King, Jr. Ave, S.E.	Washington, D.C.

Planned

Las Palmas Hotel & Residences	Las Vegas

This Project is to be a luxury resort hotel and condominium Project located on 13 acres at 3550 Paradise Boulevard in Las Vegas. Phase one of the development will consist of approximately 1 million square feet of hotel development and 130,000 SF of net sellable condominium units.

The hotel is anticipated to include approximately 100,000 SF of meeting/conference space, 10,000 SF of retail, several themed restaurants, one 3-meal restaurant, several bar/lounge areas, indoor and outdoor swimming pools, 35,000 SF luxury spa, and other amenities.

says, where "you get rewarded more for success," which is why Don Peebles came to New York in the first place.

Certainly, succeeding in New York City will not be easy, but his projects are never easy, as he has seen in his deals elsewhere. New York, however, attracts more capital from more diverse sponsors than almost any other city in the world. Like Peebles, these sponsors all want to claim a place in the world's most famous skyline, starting with the scions of the families who have been pillars of the real estate establishment in Manhattan for decades. Peebles counters their dominance by reminding a listener that the recent projects in perhaps the world's most valuable real estate market have come from those new to town and not from the stalwarts. He does acknowledge, however, that the competitive landscape may be tougher in New York, but again, that is what happens when the opportunities are more plentiful and significant and the rewards more bountiful. Hard work is expected and patience required; Peebles is capable of both. And he is quick to point out that he is not as anxious to place his mark on New York City as he is to enter into a profitable transaction.

It is probably safe to say that Don Peebles's biggest win is still ahead of him, and it will likely be in the world's most coveted neighborhood, a huge Broadway-caliber hit on the planet's biggest stage, where critical acclaim is judged by impact and profits.

The Takeaway

How does Don Peebles's way of succeeding in real estate inform the individual investor in the stock market? In fact, the Peebles way offers a blueprint for success that can be adapted to any business venture or, by extension, to any investment. It is about finding your way to the nexus of an opportunity you can leverage, dimensioning your role in the opportunity, and then limiting your risk. That pretty much sums up what Don Peebles has done, again and again, to achieve his multi-hundred-million-dollar fortune. In real estate, it is true, you can limit your risk through the participation of partners, and this may be neither possible nor desirable in building an individual stock portfolio. But the principle is what counts, and the principle of limiting your risk shows up time and again in this book precisely because it is so essential to winning big in investing.

How do you find your way to the nexus of an opportunity you can leverage? Peebles did it by keeping his eyes open. As someone brought up to see no boundaries to his own potential, he was inherently well prepared to see no boundaries to financial opportunities either. He was never

(Continued)

limited by what others couldn't imagine; in fact, you can argue that his career owes its start to someone else's lack of vision, to the $150,000 someone else didn't want to spend in a dilapidated neighborhood like Anacostia. The Miami properties, both the Royal Palm Hotel and the Bath Club, were also projects that intimidated others, but Peebles saw a way to make them workable and turned both into opportunities to earn significant return. It is as a good a lesson for the stock market as for the real estate market: Be aware of the possibilities, and don't dismiss any potential investment out of hand just because it doesn't fit the conventional wisdom; in fact, that may be a tip to take a closer look at it.

Once you've identified an opportunity, what then? The Peebles template offers important guidance here too: Define the dimension of your own role in the opportunity—your purpose and your participation. To what extent should you— and can you afford to—take part in this opportunity? By this I don't just mean how much money you invest, but also, how much time and effort you are willing to put into tracking and monitoring the investment, how long you are going to give it to realize the returns you seek, and what is the place you want the investment to take in your portfolio of assets. Peebles was ruthlessly realistic from the start about what he could and could not bring to a project, and he knew the worth of both. Similarly, in assessing a potential investment, it is important to judge it in relation to yourself—where it fits in your investing scheme and how you are going to manage it. But perhaps most critical is being honest with yourself in assessing what you know that the consensus doesn't because that will drive appreciation.

The Peebles blueprint limits the risk in an investment. In Peebles's case, he typically took half ownership of a project in compensation for the skills he brought to the table— namely: uncovering the opportunity, crafting the vision, selling it to others, and then executing as promised—essential and valuable skills, but still not everything needed to bring the project to profitable completion. Still, for Peebles, the downside was limited to his time, relatively small expenditures, and his reputation. The short term for this is "risk management," and it works when investing in the stock market as well as when undertaking a development project. Know what you can afford to lose and how much it will cost—your downside—and measure it against what you can realistically hope to gain. The reward should always be much greater then the risk.

So let's summarize the Don Peebles takeaway into a few principles that can guide your investments:

1. The point of entry into an investment should be dictated by the opportunity and the total expenditure, not by a perception of value at that point in time. In the Anacostia investment, one potential buyer walked away from the deal because he deemed the price too high. Clearly, that was a mistake. In terms of stocks, don't be put off by where the equity is trading at the time; the price may seem high but if, after performing research on the company, you can determine that the fundamentals are going to improve, then maybe the current trading price represents a bargain. Rarely should an investment opportunity be judged by how much it has returned for someone else but rather by how much upside is left for new money. Put another way, it is not where a stock has come from but where it is going to that should drive an investment decision.

2. Don't stop looking at a stock because the consensus rating by Wall Street analysts is a Sell or Hold rather than a Buy. Non-consensus thinking can lead to a *Big*

(Continued)

Win! Peebles did his own work on the Bath Club and it ultimately provided a great return. It took a lot of effort, but that is what smart investing requires. Do your own work, read what you can, research as much as you can. And, very important, do not ignore the negative view; understand the basis for the opposition in order to independently assess the investment case for the stock. Analysts tend to have a herd mentality, and going against the herd—thinking independently—can be financially rewarding. Conversely, I have made money on short positions in stocks that were universally loved by the Street where expectations were set unattainably high.

3. If you do decide to go against the consensus, do not do it because you want to *show them*. Remember, Peebles had no ego about what he did when it came to profitability. Go against the herd because you see opportunity. The glory and satisfaction will come with the win, not as a stepping-stone to it.

4. Be honest with yourself. Peebles also had no ego when assessing his own value; he was persistent in being brutally honest about his ability to impact a project. In terms of a stock, you must believe that you have an insight that others do not have into the fundamental reason for being involved. In other words, if all you know is what everyone else knows, chances are that it is a very crowded trade. That limits your upside either because there is no marginal buyer to drive the price higher, or because consensus is so widespread on the value proposition (read: the case for buying it) that losses can be significant should the story not play out according to expectations. The price will collapse as everyone seeks to sell at the same time. But if you believe the base case is X-plus instead of just X, that is likely a good enough reason to be

for your differentiated view. However, do not ever disregard the added risk of a crowded story.

5. Political connections do not come into play much for an investor in stocks, but relationships with people who are involved in sectors of the economy where you choose to invest do matter. Peebles was very well connected within Washington and was clued into the government's need for more office space. It was an insight he came to honestly and straightforwardly from being involved in the real estate market and being politically connected. Similarly, it was because he was a known entity among the brokerage community in D.C. that the broker came to him with the opportunity, and it was his knowledge of the market that gave him the confidence to meet the seller's price. As a stock investor, you should constantly chat with people who may be involved in an industry where you seek to invest. If you believe that a particular retailer represents a good stock investment, drop into the store and ask the salespeople and manager how business is. See if you can find out what they hear about the business from other managers in the company. Speak to employees in stores that compete for the same customer. This is grass-roots research, and importantly, not inside information.

6. While Peebles limited his immediate financial risk by bringing in outside investors, his reputation was at stake; had it been tarnished, that could have limited his ability to drive future transactions. Managing your risk by limiting the downside is critical to being able both to continue to invest in the market and to recoup any losses through future investments. In other words, don't invest what you can't afford to lose.

(Continued)

7. Looking at the Peebles way from the other side of the transaction, the takeaway is that allocating a portion of your investment account to a qualified money manager can be a successful strategy. Peebles started out with individual investors as his partners, eventually moving on to where he is today, with large institutional investors as the primary funding source in his transactions. The investors who have entrusted Peebles with their funds have apparently done very well. He knows that every deal can either be his last, if it fails miserably, or another opportunity to build upon his reputation. And, much like a hedge fund manager, he does not make money unless his investors profit, since his future is tied to the success of the project.

8. Make the investment your own. Do not listen to others tell you when to buy, sell, add, or decrease. It is okay to seek out advice, in fact, you should, but ultimately, as Peebles did in Miami, you have to own the investment and the decision process around it.

These principles of investing apply to all asset classes. Adhering to them can be hard work, but hard work and discipline are the primary pillars upon which Don Peebles's success rests. And they are the key lessons of the Don Peebles story.

Notes

1. The Sheraton has been converted into a Marriott. Peebles currently owns the Courtyard by Marriott Convention Center in Washington, D.C.
2. *The Peebles Interview with Steve Forbes*, Forbes.com, Intelligent Investing Briefing Book, November 14, 2008.
3. At times, Mayor Barry's image needed all the polishing it could get, since he and members of his administration were plagued by allegations of cocaine use and of corruption against his first wife and his close aides,

including one who pleaded guilty. He had his bright spots as well, with a well-received bond offering, the city's first, a place on the podium at the Democratic National Convention where he introduced Jesse Jackson as a candidate, and numerous social and development projects. Barry would ultimately serve four terms as Mayor, the last one after serving a six-month jail term for drug possession. Nonetheless, the Washington Post endorsed him for his first three terms and he won by a landslide in each election.

4. Peebles and Barry still enjoy a cordial relationship.
5. Zoning boards typically have broad powers to establish the parameters for land use. In this particular situation, the zoning board decreed that the current property could not be used for anything other than its current use as a hotel. This meant that a developer could not erect a residential property on the site.

Chapter 10

Finding Value in Junk

Martin J. Whitman

E ducation and Martin J. Whitman are closely linked.
There's the Whitman School of Management, named in his
honor, at Syracuse University, where he received the bulk of
his undergraduate education, graduating *magna cum laude* in 1949 and
topping that off, nine years later, with a Masters in economics from
the New School for Social Research in New York City.

There are the 30-plus years Whitman spent as Distinguished
Management Fellow at the Yale School of Management, along with
teaching stints at the Columbia University Graduate School of
Business and at his eponymous Whitman School.

There are the books that have become classic texts and de rigueur
reading for anyone interested in investing, security analysis, and how
not to lose your shirt in the market—*The Aggressive Conservative*

Investor and *Value Investing: A Balanced Approach*—along with numerous articles on a range of topics.

There are the lectures on securities and valuations at leading law schools and at forums and management conferences around the country.

Perhaps the commitment to education derives from Whitman's being the only son of Jewish immigrants who came to the United States from Poland in 1920, just at the tail end of that great mass migration of a people legendary for cherishing learning.

Perhaps it is because he remains grateful, in his ninth decade, for the gift of education provided by the GI Bill in return for his four years of torpor in the Navy during World War II. After enlisting in 1942, Whitman served first at an ammunition depot in Nebraska, then on an LST, (Landing Ship, Tank) vessels used in World War II to carry large vehicles and cargo and to transport troops in the Pacific. It was a term of service without any battle action but not without the development of skills. A pharmacist's mate and, he says, "a talented medic," Whitman might have gone on to medical school had he not entered into a youthful and misguided marriage. The union kept him in Nebraska after the war where he enrolled in college to prepare for work in his father-in-law's department store. He quickly exited both the marriage and Nebraska to return east—he is a New Yorker by birth and inclination—and found a place at Syracuse studying business administration, followed by a stint at Princeton for graduate study.

The profound influences of this early education are sharply recalled: a "fabulous course in Russian history" at Hastings College in Nebraska that imparted a greater understanding of the world as a whole than did all those years plying the Pacific; study at Syracuse with the great labor economist, Sidney Sufrin; "eye-opening" courses in demography at Princeton with Frank Notestein, who virtually invented the discipline, which, says Whitman, "helped me understand the way the world works"; and various courses in accounting, "the language of business." Each course of study added to the foundation of his investment philosophy.

Yet that formal instruction in those centers of education was only the beginning of what became a lifetime habit of learning. Whitman's conversation is peppered with recollections of the "great training" he received in a succession of jobs and of the "great lessons" he learned along the way. It is also peppered with critical self-assessments of his failures to understand: how he was "unbelievably stupid" when he acquired a closed-end fund named Equity Strategies in an attempt to diversify his holdings, or how he made "the wrong choice" when he joined William Blair & Co. in the late 1960s. Yet the conclusion is inescapable that, for all these self-described intellectual failures, Marty Whitman is, over a long and distinguished career, one of Wall Street's smartest, most learned, and most successful investors. Maybe the success has come because, as he himself describes it, "I focus more on what I missed—to learn from it."[1]

Educational Value Added:
On-the-Job Training

Unquestionably, Marty Whitman learned a lot and learned it well. When he left Princeton to take an entry-level job at Shearson Hamill, the much-merged brokerage house that died with Lehman Brothers, he did so because it offered "great training," assigning him first to a month on the audit desk, then one month in each back office function as background to becoming an analyst.

Analysis, the process of breaking a thing down into its constituent parts so you can see both the essential nature of the thing and how the parts relate, is something for which Whitman clearly has a knack. While working on an analysis of the timber industry, he came upon a company called M&M Woodworking and noted that it held enormous stands of timber that, in Whitman's finding, were "creating all this value while not creating any earnings." It was, he says, an "epiphany" that taught him "There are a lot more ways to create value than earnings per share." And so he became enamored with balance sheets, with understanding the true value of a company rather than just looking at what the market was according the entity in terms of valuation relative to its projected growth rate. A price-to-earnings multiple does not take into account non-income producing assets, even though they may add to growth in the future or possess more current value than what the market believes the company is worth based on some other metric.

Whitman's penchant for analysis and his obvious skill at it, bolstered by all that education, had little room to maneuver at Shearson, a classic wire-house brokerage that simply did not deal in independent research. Even when Whitman went to the underwriting side of the shop because it was a "chance to do more in-depth analysis," he was disappointed in the level of research he could do. Much of the due diligence, he recalls, "was mostly a fake. A hot issue sold itself, the 'analysis' essentially just confirming that it was hot." So Whitman moved to the family office of the celebrated investor and philanthropist, William Rosenwald, where, under the mentorship of senior analysts, he got a chance to hone his skills and to learn first-hand about control investing, risk management, and the kind of analysis both require. It was simple, says Whitman. Rosenwald and the principals "cared about what they were buying because it was their money." They were therefore very careful to learn all that could be learned before buying anything.

He then moved to Ladenburg Thalmann Financial Services Inc., which was a smaller firm that also invested its partners' money, as well as that of a few clients. Whitman was Head of Research and "followed everything"—every sector and every industry where profitable investments might be found. He remembers doing an analysis of R.J. Reynolds Tobacco and coming upon "some kind of Surgeon General's report"—the year was 1958 or 1959—and Whitman, a heavy smoker since his Navy days, immediately quit his smoking habit "cold turkey." He was not just ahead of his time; he was and is a man who researches deeply and pays attention to what he finds—the lifetime learning habit in action.

A colleague at Ladenburg persuaded Whitman to move to Philadelphia to join a firm called Gerstley Sunstein as a partner in charge of research. The Whitmans—he had married again by this time, and the couple had three young children—stayed in Philadelphia until 1967 before the siren song of New York summoned them home, and it was then that Whitman made "the wrong choice" and joined the New York office of William Blair & Co.

It was the wrong choice because at that point in its history, the venerable Chicago-based firm, in Whitman's words, "ran a really terrible operation. . . . The retail business was awful, and they failed to participate in the IPO boom in the late 1960s, when they should have become managing underwriters." Whitman "stood it" for a few years, but in 1970 he decided to go out on his own.

Solo

He "really liked corporate finance" and was "firmly committed to value investing up to this point," asserts Whitman. "Value investing is just passive investing." But he was learning that there are "related fields," as he puts it, in which "the same variables were at work": control investing, distressed investing, credit analysis, and first and second stage venture capital. Since Whitman sees himself as "basically an analyst, not a manager," he claims no interest in the last of these related fields, but has an abiding interest in the others. By 1972, he had begun teaching about them at Yale.

At the same time, he began to be retained in an advisory capacity in Chapter 10-type bankruptcy cases by trustees or creditors, and he found himself increasingly in demand as an expert witness in bankruptcy litigation—first for plaintiffs, then eventually for defendant corporations. Thanks to his background, says Whitman—especially to his time in a wire house—"I knew where the earnings maturity came from; I could understand what people were doing."

He incorporated the business in 1975 as M. J. Whitman & Co. a fairly optimistic title for a business consisting, at the time, of Whitman and his secretary, Marilyn Haynsworth. A couple of salesmen came on board, but the brokerage was really a small part of the business, concentrating on bankruptcy and stockholder litigation which were "two great training areas," as Whitman labels them. He built up "a pretty good practice," claiming as one of his clients the U.S. government when he became the principal financial advisor to the Department of Justice's antitrust division. In that role he did "a lot of the work-outs for pension and benefit guarantee corporations." This experience would prove to be invaluable.

Toward the end of the 1970s, however, Whitman decided to "concentrate more on being an investor." After all, he had the education, and now he had all that great training. His first big score came when he was approached by some mortgage bondholders in the Penn Central bankruptcy (see the section "Bringing the Carcass Back to Life," further on)—at that time, the biggest bankruptcy in U.S. history. Whitman's investment in retained asset bonds "did very well in the reorganization" and became only the first of his many successful investments in distressed businesses.

Since distress "is a confrontational business," in Whitman's term—he distinguishes it from Mergers & Acquisitions, which he calls "a lover's business"—he decided to diversify and seek control of a closed-end investment company.[2] In 1984, he bought up the common stock of a small closed-end fund called Equity Strategies Fund Inc., and he entered the asset management business.

It seemed a smart move. After all, Whitman wanted control, and he got it. And he pursued what was becoming his trademark investing thesis—safe and cheap—with a record that markedly outperformed the market over the long term. Yet Whitman calls himself "unbelievably stupid" in taking over Equity Strategies—not because it was not a good thing to do, but because he had not seen the real value in control. "The real wealth," he says, was not in buying at a discount but rather "in inheriting the management contract."

"Having a management company is better than running the tolls on the George Washington Bridge," says Marty Whitman in his famously gritty voice, still inflected with the sounds of the Bronx boy he once was. "It's all cash. *You're* the overhead. There's no inventory. No credit risk." Whitman took over Equity Strategies, open-ended it, and used it to get control of other companies, mostly through bankruptcy reorganizations. The bankruptcy consulting morphed into the investment banking firm Whitman, Heffernan, Rhein and Co. It was the start of the activist control investing for which he is so famous, and the watchword of Whitman's kind of investing became "safe, cheap, and with a seat at the table."

There was a succession of big wins: Mission Insurance Company, Covanta Energy, K-Mart, Brookfield Asset Management. Along with his Princeton classmate Eugene Isenberg, Whitman did the second pre-packaged bankruptcy reorganization[3] ever for a company called Anglo Energy. The reorganized company took the name Nabors Industries, into which Equity Strategies's assets were eventually merged—an enormous win for Equity Strategies shareholders. Nabors has become a very well respected company in the energy services sector with a market capitalization in excess of $5 billion. Whitman is Director Emeritus while Eisenberg retains his title as Chairman of the Board of Directors.

By this time, says Whitman, he had decided to put down stakes in the mutual fund business—in his words, he "figured out that mutual funds are a license to steal"—so in 1990, he launched the Third Avenue Value Fund, starting "with a few million." By 1997, Third Avenue had more than a billion dollars in assets under management. How did it happen? Says Whitman, perhaps too modestly: "I really don't know. I don't know how we built assets and got clients. But I do know that in growing these businesses, performance is nowhere nearly as important as trust and good services."

The More You Know . . .

"The best thing that ever happened to the mutual fund industry," says Marty Whitman, "is the Participant Disclosure Regulation."[4] The reason? "So the public knows we don't cheat them." It is why Whitman has made "the highest degree of integrity" the hallmark of Third Avenue Value Fund. Think about it: Integrity is the corollary of the Whitman commitment to education. The more you know, the better off you will be.

The firm is famous for its simple and singular approach, what its website refers to as the "one proven value philosophy" that guides the firm's investing—namely, "safe companies that are cheaply priced." Whitman lays down four criteria for choosing equities in which to invest. The business must:

1. Provide comprehensive disclosure in plain language with reliable audits.
2. Have a super-strong financial position.
3. Represent an opportunity to buy in at a very large discount from a readily ascertainable net asset value.
4. Possess excellent prospects for growing its readily ascertainable net asset value over the next three to five years at much better than 10 percent compounded.

The balance sheet is the key focus of bottom-up analysis to determine if a company meets these criteria, with a focus on the quality and quantity of existing resources rather than on future projections. But current financial strengths are not the only measure looked at in Third Avenue's search for bargains, especially since "safe" counts for more than "cheap"; note that safety comprises three of Whitman's four criteria. He stays safe by being price-conscious—buying growth and asset but not paying full value; by looking at long-term investment risk, not market risk; and by learning everything it is possible to learn about a company before investing in it—and continuing to stay on top of the fundamentals once it has joined the ranks of his holdings. No one indicator can tell it all; comprehensive, rigorous analysis is required.

Retail investors make mistakes, says Whitman, when they "don't understand the business or the securities or are short-term conscious. But you can only make out as a retail investor by trying to guard against investment risk, not against market risk," and that means becoming a student of what you are investing in. Only that kind of study, Whitman argues, can illumine for the investor the choices that are both safe and "real cheap." It is a discipline his funds have "never consciously violated," and while he is certain the discipline has been unintentionally violated, he is also certain that such violations have always been a mistake.

To be sure, there are not that many stocks that meet the Whitman criteria, and for those that do, it often takes a considerable period of time to unlock the value. So patience and the long view are qualities Whitman has perfected. His quarterly letters to shareholders reflect both and are as charmingly blunt as the man himself is in person. Still holding the title of Chairman, Whitman remains a formidable presence at Third Avenue Fund's headquarters, although it is probably fair to say he spends less time at work than he used to. He has other interests. His wife, Lois, founded the children's rights division of Human Rights Watch and remains its Director. Whitman has philanthropic pursuits as well—most notably to his alma mater, Syracuse University, and to affirmative action programs for Arab students in Israeli schools. The commitment to education—and seeing to it that others get the same shot he was given—persist.

Bringing the Carcass Back to Life

Whitman is a man of values who made his career seeking value in companies that were given up for dead by others. His first real foray into vulture investing, that is, buying the "distressed" bonds of companies that are in financial straits, often in bankruptcy, was the fabled but poorly managed Penn Central Transportation Company. In 1968, the Pennsylvania Railroad and the New York Central Railroad merged, hoping to eliminate redundancies in their coal hauling businesses that operated in Ohio, West Virginia, the long eastern seaboard route, and New York. On paper, it wasn't a bad idea, but a weakening economy, inept management, and stubborn union leadership unwittingly joined together to drive the company into bankruptcy, creating the first major event for what would be a new class of investors.

As with most areas of the law, bankruptcy is one that requires a special expertise. The written law and the case law are just two of the many different facets of this intricate transaction. Add the fact that railroads are a highly regulated industry, and the inscrutability grows substantially, as one would expect any time the government is involved. In this particular case, the government had an even more acute interest in the transaction because transportation is so critical to the country's economic health and security. This increased complexity would work to Whitman's benefit; he not only knew his way around the bankruptcy courts and statutes, having already been a consultant and expert witness for a number of years, he also had experience in litigation matters involving the government. The bottom line: If anyone could navigate the ins and outs of this bankruptcy, it was Marty Whitman. That group of creditors—mortgage bondholders—certainly thought so; they found Whitman's resume so attractive that they hired him as their representative in the Penn Central bankruptcy proceedings.

Vulture investing was just becoming an investment class when Penn Central went belly-up. Most bankruptcy situations up to that time were significantly smaller in terms of publicly traded debt, but the profit potential inherent in the sheer size of this, the largest bankruptcy anyone had ever seen, attracted a number of new players. Where they saw profit potential, and why creditors looked to Whitman to get it for them, requires a bit of explanation.

Start with the fact that bondholders tend to be more risk-averse than owners of stock in a corporation. They prefer to take their yield in the form of steady interest payments rather than seeking significant appreciation in the price of the investment. However, while bond prices do fluctuate, the fluctuation usually hovers within a significantly tighter range than with stocks; the terminal upside at maturity of a bond is limited to par, while a stock can theoretically trade to infinity. But what can go up, can go down, and in the case of equity, the downside in a bankruptcy is almost always zero. Bondholders, however, have a claim against the assets of a company and most often receive partial payment; the value of the bonds during a bankruptcy proceeding is diminished in value since the interest, or coupon, is no longer paid and because the ultimate recovery is uncertain. This being the case, the traditional fixed income investor, a conservative sort to begin with, looks for an out since it is often beyond their purview to hold a distressed instrument; they often lack the expertise or mandate to perform an analysis that will show that these troubled bonds may ultimately be worth more in a bankruptcy workout than under fire sale terms. Thus, their only real option is to sell and this is where Marty Whitman entered the picture with Penn Central.[5]

A company going through bankruptcy proceedings, guided by its lawyers, must present a plan for either winding down its business or reorganizing and exiting the process as a viable ongoing concern. Nowadays, by the time this plan is presented, distressed investors have usually acquired all the bonds, having hired their own team of attorneys and analysts to assess how much meat is left on the carcass. But since vulture investing was still a relatively new phenomenon in the case of Penn Central, the due diligence process was not as sophisticated. That did not stop Marty Whitman. On the contrary, he believed, rightly, that it favored him; it provided the advantage of a less efficient market and provided the opportunity for bigger profits. On behalf of the creditors who retained him, he waded into the mess and liked what he saw.

While others were scared into selling their bonds, the words *"wiped out"* looming large in their thoughts, Whitman pored over the plan of reorganization. He saw tremendous value in the documents filed by the company with their lists of real estate and business interests that had been pledged as collateral for the bonds and that were unencumbered by the railroad's problems. No one really wants the government involved in their business, but the government's insinuation into this process—in 1973, Congress had voted to nationalize the bankrupt railroad—would turn out to be the best thing to happen to Whitman and the other vulture investors. The takeover left all non-transportation assets, including the real estate, in the parent company. This real estate was what attracted Whitman to Penn Central because the property was used as collateral for the mortgage bonds he would own. Whitman bought $100,000 worth of the seemingly near-worthless securities, a rather large investment at the time and under the circumstances. It took about a year for the court to approve the reorganization plan, but with a profit of five times his investment, Whitman was paid well to wait.

The Takeaway

Marty Whitman did not invent vulture investing, or as it has more recently been termed—and with greater social acceptability—distressed investing. Nor did he invent value investing, which operates along the same principles but with practical applicability to many more types of securities. But he did pioneer the strategy of distressed investing and brought fresh thinking to the way value investing was approached. In essence, what Whitman defined, refined, and taught through his lectures at Yale and his three books[6] was the process of value investing, however strong the vital signs of the prospective investment. And that is no simple matter. Too often reduced to the simplistic notion of finding a stock that appears cheap or on sale, value investing in Whitman's view, and as his career evidences, is serious business, one requiring—not surprisingly for Whitman—serious study. And it can be a minefield.

Some investments that are bought on price dislocation alone wind up being "value traps." Value traps are best defined as securities that appear cheap but actually are not; in other words, the price reflects the value of the current fundamentals rather than a discount to its value as a business. For example, during the dot-com bubble, many Internet stocks declined significantly in price, providing an opportunity along the way for price-conscious investors to snap up shares. Yahoo! provides a perfect illustration. The stock price peaked on a split-adjusted basis at $125 per share in March 2000. Over the course of the next year, the price declined, ultimately bottoming at below $5.00 a share. I am quite sure that investors all along the way looked at the price and said something to the effect of "Wow! Yahoo! is trading at $100, 20 percent off its high. That's cheap!" Fast forward, but not too fast because if you do, you will miss the point in time when another buyer exclaimed: "Wow! I can buy Yahoo! for $60 a share, less than half of what it cost six months ago. Now that is cheap!" And so it went. But here is the question: Despite the stock price, was it ever really cheap? I would say not until it hit the bottom. As the price declined, the fundamentals worsened and the valuation umbrella—that is, the overall Price to Earnings ratio of the market (and other quantitative measures) failed to support the price. AOL became a stronger competitor—at least for a time; Ask.com sprang up; and ultimately Google slammed Yahoo!'s competitive position and business model to smithereens. The following illustration makes this point: A company, whose equity is trading at $100, has provided earnings guidance of ten dollars a share equating to a P/E multiple of 10X. A month later the management revises

(*Continued*)

guidance to five dollars and the stock trades down on this news to $75, a decline of 25 percent. Despite the steep decline in price, the stock has actually become more expensive since the P/E multiple is now 15X.

The point is that if someone had bought shares entirely based on the supposition that they *appeared* cheap during the decline relative to where the stock price had peaked, that individual may become snared in a good old value trap in which the securities were not as inexpensive as they seemed. Marty Whitman would not have fallen into such a trap. What looks cheap may actually prove expensive once you educate yourself about the other factors that form part of any value proposition. The other factors clearly at play in the Yahoo! situation went to the heart of the company's ability to compete, its business model, and its expected growth in revenues and earnings. Safety as well as price: the Marty Whitman mantra.

So how should you assess value and not get caught in a less than valuable situation or in a situation where the company is insolvent, thus erasing any possible recovery in bankruptcy? The first step, but only the first step, is to look at the valuation based upon where the stock is presently trading rather than at where it *was* trading. Use multiple valuation measures for that industry—not as an arbitrage against the market but rather as an insight into the company as a business.

That is what value investors and Marty Whitman do. They ignore the stock market, and they ignore interest rate and GDP forecasts. Rather, value analysis focuses purely on a particular company's business prospects, deployment of and return on capital, industry positioning, balance sheet, management—well, you get the picture. Value investors are the first responders to troubled situations, more willing than others to dig deep and assess the intrinsic value of a company before it attracts others. There are art dealers who can find the genuine folk primitive painting in a flea market full of tacky junk, mechanics who can see the potential in damaged machinery, and investors who can discern value in companies that have taken a wrong turn or suffered a misstep. And because those investors come to that judgment early, they have to be patient while the company works through its issues. As the business improves, so does the appeal to other investors, and this is when the payoff begins.

So how can the average investor participate in distressed investing, one of the more esoteric areas of capital markets? It is not easy. Ideally, the most basic requirement for successful distressed investing is a very strong analytical background steeped in corporate capital structure; a legal background or access to such resources would also be very helpful. You will need that if you are going to sort through the myriad documents that lay out the seniority of each security and what each class of investor would be entitled to in any recovery in bankruptcy or corporate reorganization. While bonds are senior to equities, there are different levels of seniority within the debt structure, including those that are collateralized by property—such as the mortgage bonds in the Penn Central bankruptcy. Obviously, that's a tall order. Owning all the skills and knowledge that enable an investor to sufficiently analyze distressed debt situations is probably beyond the capabilities and resources of most individual investors. But there are other options—namely, participating in distressed investing through a mutual fund or a hedge fund. Of course, as with any investment, check the performance of the fund and make sure the risk parameters fit with your particular goals and means. For more on how Marty Whitman chooses stocks, see Table 10.1.

Table 10.1 Whitman's Criteria for Choosing Stocks

- Comprehensive disclosure in plain language with reliable audits
- A super-strong financial position
- We must be able to buy in at a very large discount from a readily ascertainable net asset value
- The business must have excellent prospects for being able to grow its readily ascertainable net asset value over the next three to five years at much better than 10 percent compounded

The Corporate Capital Structure: Bonds and Equities

Why do people invest in corporate bonds versus stocks? First let's define our terms.

The corporate bond universe is composed of two categories of bonds: investment-grade and non-investment grade. The latter are also called high-yield bonds or junk bonds, a term that is not as pejorative to bond traders as it seems to be to the layman. Bonds that are rated below BBB by Standard & Poor's and below Baa by Moody's are considered non-investment grade. The companies that issue these bonds pay investors a higher interest rate—thus the term "high-yield"—as an inducement, compensation to the bond buyer for assuming a greater risk of default. As with investment-grade bonds, not all high-yield paper carries the same rating; some issuances are riskier than others. There is no similar rating system for equities.

A typical investor in stocks, particularly a momentum or growth stock investor, is usually less concerned about a company's balance sheet than an investor in the credit of a company although both should have the same concerns.

Ultimately, all the credit investor really cares about is whether the interest on the debt will be paid. But the bondholder also wants to know that in the event there is not enough cash flow to pay the interest on the debt, the company's assets have as value that exceeds the price they paid for the bonds.

High-yield bonds are a different animal and require more balance sheet and cash flow analysis than investment-grade bonds. This is because, by definition, their financial situation and business prospects are more tenuous. It is these companies that are significantly more likely to fall into bankruptcy.

Value investors use balance sheet and cash flow analysis in a manner more or less consistent with that of high-yield bond investors because they are both dealing with impaired entities. Junk bonds are balance sheet impaired; value stocks may have strong balance sheets, but their business model has likely taken a hit. In the case of an equity, the investor generally wants assurance that the company will remain a going concern and that the parts are worth more than the whole; that is, the investor seeks assurance that were the company to be sold as a single entity or its assets sold off individually, the sale would fetch more than the current stock price. Bond investors, on the other hand, don't care about the stock price; they only care about the proceeds of a sale being sufficient to redeem the bonds at the price they paid for them, which may or may not be the face value.

In the Penn Central example, bondholders like Marty Whitman were paid face value, while equity holders were basically wiped out. Once the bonds were redeemed, no assets remained.

Notes

1. Whitman is not alone in deliberating over his mistakes, using them as a valuable learning experience for his future investment activities. This is the premise of *The Billion Dollar Mistake*, my first book.

2. A closed-end investment company issues a finite number of shares, which are listed on a stock exchange. The size of the fund rises and falls with the value of its underlying investments as does the stock price. This differs from an open-end investment company that continually issues and redeems its shares. As more money comes into the fund, more shares are issued and it grows larger. Conversely, as shares are redeemed the fund becomes smaller.

3. Prepackaged bankruptcy reorganization: a plan for the financial reorganization of a company that is prepared and voted on by shareholders before the bankruptcy petition is filed. This plan is negotiated with creditors of the company and becomes effective once the company is officially in bankruptcy. Because the plan is already negotiated with creditors and approved by shareholders, the process for emerging from bankruptcy protection is less expensive and shorter.

4. The Participant Disclosure Regulation is also called the Participant Fee Disclosure Regulation. It requires that fees paid by or to various organizations such as investment advisors, plan sponsors, and mutual funds must be disclosed to plan participants and mutual fund investors. These regulations have been continually revised and their application broadened since first enacted.

5. As junk bond investing increased in popularity, it grew into its own asset class. Relative to the entire fixed income industry, very few funds actually invest in both investment grade and non-investment grade, or junk, bonds.

6. Martin J. Whitman and Martin Shubik, *The Aggressive Conservative Investor* (Hoboken, NJ: John Wiley & Sons, 2005); Martin J. Whitman and Fernando Diaz, *Distress Investing: Principles and Technique* (Hoboken, NJ: John Wiley & Sons, 2009); Martin J. Whitman, *Value Investing: A Value Approach* (New York: John Wiley & Sons, 2000).

7. An investor in the credit of a company is an investor in the company's bonds. Bondholders are creditors since they have effectively loaned the company money. Bondholders are, of course, first in line for recovery in the event of the liquidation of a company since all debts must be repaid before an equity shareholder receives anything. While equity investors should be more concerned with a company's debt structure, they often are not, particularly growth stock investors, since high growth companies usually do not have significant amounts of outstanding debt.

Conclusion: So There You Have It . . .

Legendary investors, brilliant business people—what do they have in common and what can you learn from them? The first thing to understand is that each of these individuals is an entrepreneur. Merriam-Webster defines entrepreneur as: "one who organizes, manages, and assumes the risks of a business or enterprise."[1] I know what you may be thinking—the guy who started XYZ Software Company is an entrepreneur. Buying a few stocks and bonds every now and then is hardly comparable to owning a business; it's just not the same. I maintain that this type of narrow thinking is the problem with the way numerous investors approach the market. Consider the parallels: Entrepreneurs and investors share a common goal which is to generate exponential return on an investment while limiting loss. For the former, it is in terms of a greater value to their enterprise; for investors it is the same exact goal except

211

that their enterprise is their portfolio. And the same decision process should be in control: How much capital has to be put at risk to earn a reasonable return, and does the specific potential for loss make the investment worthwhile?

There are many different types of entrepreneurs, and creating a new website from your college dorm room is only one way to build a business. No one can deny that hedge fund managers are entrepreneurial, as are private wealth managers. In fact, so are individual investors except they have only themselves as clients. The point is that both the money manager and the software genius have each started a business that is based upon generating return from financial instruments. Investing in stocks is a business, and by extension, each time you invest in a stock, you should be assessing the fundamentals of each company whose shares you are considering in the same way a venture capital or private equity investor sizes up an opportunity.

Prior to starting a business, the entrepreneur will look at the competitive landscape, assessing the opportunity for differentiating his business model. The next decision is whether the risk of investment in the business justifies the potential reward, handicapping both outcomes. The stock investor should do the same. Is Coca-Cola better positioned than Pepsi, or is there enough room for both to meet their targets? Based upon the share price and valuation metrics, what is the potential downside, what is the upside? These are business decisions, strictly business decisions. And this is why Chuck Royce, for example, says that he buys companies, not stocks. So the common threads that run through each of the previous chapters include the following five principles to which investors should adhere:

1. A defined and clearly articulated investment strategy.
2. Introspection—the marriage of experience and bias with investment style.
3. The discipline never to stray from a defined strategy.
4. A strict risk discipline.
5. A detachment from emotion; clear and unemotional analysis.

So there you have it: Becoming a successful investor is not about following well-known or legendary investors into a trade for, as with life, the end does not always justify the means. Instead, focus on the strategy and process that the well-known investor's reputation is based upon and adjust it to your own strengths. Develop a repeatable, reliable process and you dramatically increase your probability of success. This is the takeaway.

Give a man a fish and you feed him for a day. Teach a man to fish and you feed him for a lifetime.

Note

1. www.merriam-webster.com/dictionary/entrepreneur.

About the Author

Stephen L. Weiss is the Managing Partner of Short Hills Capital Partners, LLC. He is an active investor, markets expert, public speaker, and the author of the top selling *The Billion Dollar Mistake: Learning the Art of Investing Through the Missteps of Legendary Investors* (John Wiley & Sons, 2010). In addition to the English language version, it is available in two Chinese dialects, Vietnamese, Korean, and Japanese. A 25-year veteran of Wall Street, he has held senior management positions at Salomon Brothers, SAC Capital, and Lehman Brothers, where he built Wall Street's #1 ranked sales force. Weiss is a CNBC Contributor with a regular role on *Fast Money* and the *Fast Money Halftime Report*. Additionally, he frequently appears on *The Kudlow Report* and other CNBC shows. *The Big Win: Learning from the Legends to Become a More Successful Investor* is his second investment book. He has also written *Hedged,* a novel about *A Killing in the Market.* Due to be released in 2012, it is a financial thriller.

Weiss maintains strong relationships with some of the industry's most highly regarded investment managers. He is a former tax attorney and a member of the American Bar Association. The author resides in New Jersey with his wife Lauren, daughters Shelby and Lindsay, and three dogs: Dino, Pebbles, and Fred.

You can visit www.stephenlweiss.com to learn more about the author.

Index